Subterranean Britain
COLD WAR BUNKERS

Subterranean Britain
COLD WAR BUNKERS

Nick Catford

FOLLY BOOKS

Folly Books 2010

© Nick Catford 2010

A catalogue record for this book is available from the British Library.

ISBN 978-0-9564405-2-5

Published by Folly Books Ltd
Monkton Farleigh
BA15 2QP
www.follybooks.co.uk

Designed and typeset by Vicky

Printed and bound in Great Britain by J F Print Ltd, Sparkford

Introductory and jacket photographs

Facing title page: The ROC No.7 Group, Bedford, control bunker at Biddenham in Bedfordshire. The bunker was demolished in 2000.

Front jacket: The Central Government War Headquarters at Corsham. This view, taken near the bottom of passenger lift PL1, shows the main access roads to Areas 3 and 4.

Back jacket: Interior view of the Linesman L1 control centre at West Drayton.

CONTENTS

Dedication

I would like to dedicate this book to the memory of Dan McKenzie, who accompanied me on many of my bunker visits and thought nothing of driving from Peterborough to Ayr and back, or from Peterborough to Land's End and back, in a single day.

Chapter 1

INTRODUCTION

Although from its title one might think this volume is perhaps a military or political history of the Cold War, it is, in fact, essentially a book concerned solely with modern day archaeology – pictures of the recent past, obscure structures that survive in (or more frequently under) the British landscape; secret structures that were seemingly essential to Britain's survival for a relatively brief period but which have since, for the most part, slipped quietly into oblivion.

Any book of this sort ought to begin with a brief explanation of the origins of the Cold War, but to attempt to do this in a paragraph or two is an invitation to criticism and derision from every tint and shade of the political spectrum. As you have already opened this book the probability is that you already have a fair depth of knowledge of, and a fairly well entrenched opinion as to the causes of, the Cold War. A few lines here will not change your opinion and it is certainly not my intention to attempt to do so. The cause, anyway, is immaterial; the fact is that tensions arose in the immediate aftermath of the Second World War between two nations: the United States and the Soviet Union. Nations with radically different cultures and economic ideologies, on opposite sides of the political divide and opposite sides of the world, they felt mutually threatened and, however laughable it may seem now, took what they thought at the time was appropriate action. Both sides were armed with atomic and, later, nuclear weapons, so it was clear from the start that any armed conflict would be more than just a little local difficulty.

Britain immediately found herself in the midst of this simmering altercation between these far away nations of which she knew enough to understand that things could very well get quite nasty pretty quickly. Ideologically and, because of her colossal war debts, economically, tied to the apron strings of the United States, she was, in the words of the journalist Duncan Campbell, soon pushed into the role of America's unsinkable aircraft-carrier. Unfortunately this role was not adopted entirely unwillingly. Britain in the 1950s suffered irrational delusions of grandeur. The majority view within the country, moulded by constant propaganda, was that she had single-handedly won the Second World War despite the inconvenient intervention of the United States and the Soviet Union; her industrialists and financiers still maintained the illusion that Britain was the workshop of the world despite the fact that her industrial dominance was already in decline by the time of the Great Exhibition of 1851 and had inexorably slipped further from her grasp with every passing year. Worst of all, the British government could not relinquish the fiction that they had command of an Empire that encircled the globe and upon which the sun never set. Close identification with the interests of the United States might have been forced upon Britain by economic necessity but was also embraced in desperation by a nation that hoped, by so doing, to maintain a position at the top table of international diplomacy that it perhaps did not unquestionably deserve.

Subjected to her own inflated military and diplomatic ambition, which envisaged the continued projection of military power across the globe, and with the British Isles acting as host to multi-faceted elements of America's forward defence policy – not just atomic bombers based on East Anglian airfields, but also long-range radar and strategic communications systems, intelligence establishments and missiles which, while nominally British were in fact under the absolute control of the United States - the nation, its institutions and its entire population were exposed to the imminent threat of nuclear annihilation. To counter this threat Britain became the most densely enbunkered nation in the world.

During the early 1950s new and refurbished wartime radar stations, each with an underground or semi-underground bomb-proof control bunker, proliferated around the southern and eastern coastlines. To operate in conjunction with these a series of new hardened Anti-Aircraft Operations Rooms were constructed to control batteries of medium and heavy guns in thirty-three Gun Defended Areas utilising, for the most part, existing wartime gun sites in proximity to the most strategically important industrial cities and ports. Meanwhile, a new network of bunkers emerged for an invigorated post-war Civil Defence force fit for the atomic age; and heavily protected and self-sufficient Regional War Rooms – twelve throughout the provinces with four more for Greater London – were built to house the Regional Commissioners and their staffs who would oversee the government of the nation should communication with London be lost.

In little more than five years most of this infrastructure would be obsolete and redundant. The radar stations, the mainstay of the Rotor programme, were designed to offer defence against relatively slow-flying Russian bombers carrying either conventional or atomic bombs and their mode of operation was based upon the complex and time-wasting control and reporting procedures that evolved, with radar technology itself, during the Second World War. The advent of high-speed, high-altitude bombers by the mid-1950s marked the end of the anti-aircraft guns and their associated operations rooms, all of which were decommissioned in March 1955. Similarly, the increase in aircraft speeds exposed the weakness of the existing radar control and reporting system. The laborious, two-stage, landline re-transmission of track data via the Sector Operations Centres was simply too slow and was a factor in the decision to abandon them in 1958. The initial implementation of the Rotor programme was, from the start, seen as an interim measure that would suffice until a more advanced system, then little more than a twinkle in the eye of the putative defence electronics industry, came to fruition towards the end of the decade. An unexpected breakthrough in 10cm radar research led to the introduction of a highly successful interim system, later known as Type 80, which entered service from 1954. Improvements to the Type 80 radar rendered it suitable for both the tracking and intercept functions and this, along with other advances in data handling, aided the demise of the Sector Operations Centres in 1958. Type 80 and its successors threw the Rotor programme somewhat into disarray with many sites becoming immediately redundant and others requiring considerable modification. By the end of the decade, however, manned bombers had been superseded by nuclear-armed ballistic missiles against which no defence was possible and almost the whole Rotor system was abandoned. Over the following thirty years a few stations, notably those at Buchan, Boulmer and Neatishead, have been reconfigured as Control and Reporting Centres under various subsequent UK air defence plans, but the majority were simply abandoned. The legacy was a huge stock of hardened underground bunkers – the most secure and bomb-proof structures ever built in Britain – many of which were never used again. A few, however, found alternative Cold War functions and their stories can be found below.

The Regional War Rooms fared little better. Conceived in 1951, they were designed to fulfil what was a essentially a Second World War civil defence rescue and recovery role which was at odds with the reality of nuclear war. In the early 1950s the effects of the atomic bomb and its mode of use were envisaged in terms of it being no more than an extraordinarily powerful conventional bomb. City centres were its targets, widespread and severe blast damage were its consequences, and the concept of radioactive fallout was little understood. Hence, the War Rooms were generally built on the outskirts of major conurbations and were substantial, blast-proof buildings from where the local rescue and recovery effort would be co-ordinated while the inevitable, short-term social dislocation persisted. The advent of nuclear weapons required a completely different rationale. The magnitude of destruction would be so immense that short-term rescue and recovery would be an irrelevance and, while the initial damage by blast and fire would be immediate and catastrophic, the effects of radiation and of comprehensive social breakdown posed the most intractable problems in the medium term. What was required was not a bomb-proof headquarters with a small staff oriented towards conventional civil defence, but a much larger, fallout-protected centre – a true Regional Seat of Government – from which all aspects of civil government could be exercised autonomously for a prolonged period.

The problem was that government's idea of what it did *not* want in terms of civil contingency planning was somewhat more advanced than that for what it *did* want, and what it did want it could not afford in conjunction with other aspects of the defence budget, notably the development of its own atomic arsenal. As a consequence, for a decade or so a host of largely obscure new schemes and modified schemes were drawn up for the provision of Regional Seats of Government and Sub-Regional Controls, under various guises, to ease the administrative burden on the primary centres. Many remained un-built, some are assumed to have maintained shadowy existences within the secure boundaries of various military establishments, a few squatted in the basements of contemporary government office blocks, but most, due to budgetary restrictions, made use of earlier structures from disparate eras, cobbled together to function, after a fashion. At Nottingham and Cambridge the Regional War Rooms were extended and adapted while elsewhere, long-abandoned Second World War underground locations found a new lease of life. At Drakelow in the West Midlands parts of a wartime underground factory were converted, as was another smaller example built in a chalk mine at Warren Row near Reading. The latter achieved some notoriety when its secrets were exposed by *Spies for Peace* in April 1963. At much the same time a much larger underground factory at Spring Quarry near Corsham in Wiltshire became the Central Government War Headquarters – the alternate seat of government to which the Great and the Good would decamp in the event of a nuclear war. The very existence of the site was denied by the Government for decades. When its secrets were finally revealed in December 2005 it proved to be a grave disappointment. Starved of cash by successive administrations, its development had been halting and, despite its enormous size, the Spring Quarry site is bathed in a gloomy aura of half-hearted compromise.

Two other wartime sites, at Brackla near Bridgend in South Wales and at Swynnerton in Staffordshire were, at different times, incorporated into the regional government schemes. Both were on the sites of former Royal Ordnance Factories and both involved the conversion of adjacent pairs of underground explosives magazines to provide the necessary space. The vast array of now abandoned Rotor bunkers and associated Anti-Aircraft Operations Rooms offered the most attractive pool of potential RSG sites and many, over subsequent decades, were converted for this, or for use as local authority control centres or for other purposes. All, however, were to some extent ad hoc structures; none were built specifically to perform the functions required of them. Such facilities, indeed, would not exist until the dying days of the Cold War when the new Conservative government under Margaret Thatcher initiated the construction of a series of multi-million-pound purpose-built Regional Government Headquarters including the examples illustrated in this book at Ballymena, Chilmark and Cultybraggan.

A prevalent theme of civil contingency planning in Britain throughout the Cold War was the shedding of responsibility for most administrative functions to increasingly lower tiers of the government hierarchy. Thus, Central Government quickly devolved responsibility for all roles except the prosecution of the war and relations with foreign powers to the Regional Commissioners who, in turn, devolved most of their responsibilities upon the local authority emergency organisations. At that point the system more or less broke down because throughout the country local authority provision at county and district levels was decidedly patchy and erratic. Some counties embraced their responsibilities with vigour, others less so, while a large minority merely paid lip-service or prepared paper plans that they had little intention of putting into

practice. Council responsibility for the re-energized post-war Civil Defence organisation drifted opaquely into a broader emergency planning role, and left a litter of small abandoned bunkers behind it. In some counties disused Anti-Aircraft Operations Rooms were pressed back into service as County Controls and Sub-Controls; in others, sophisticated modern control centres were incorporated into the basements of new-built civic centres, council headquarters, libraries and old-people's homes. Elsewhere, including in a number of London boroughs, dilapidated old Civil Defence headquarters remained the only provision.

Numerically, the organisation that littered the landscape with the largest crop of abandoned bunkers was the Royal Observer Corps. Stood down in May 1945, the Observer Corps was brought back to life just eighteen months later to help fill the many holes in the RAF's post-war radar coverage. In 1951 the Corps was provided with new concrete 'Orlit' observation posts built to a standard design to replace the ad hoc assortment that had survived the war, and which offered a modicum of weather-proofing along with relatively unimpeded views of the sky. Shortly afterwards, the role of the Corps was more tightly integrated with the Rotor radar system. 1955 saw the formation of the United Kingdom Warning and Monitoring Organisation (UKWMO) whose task it was to give warning of a nuclear attack and monitor the paths of subsequent fallout clouds. Although nominally an independent organisation UKWMO shared much of the ROC infrastructure and established five sector controls in existing ROC headquarters. The arrival of UKWMO also precipitated the provision of some 1,563 reasonably blast and radiation-proof underground monitoring posts and thirty-one (later reduced to twenty-nine) new Group Headquarters bunkers. Just three years later a funding crisis led to the abandonment of 686 of the underground posts and two Group Headquarters at Watford and Leeds. The whole organisation was closed down at the end of March, 1992 although two Group Headquarters remained in use for some time as Nuclear Reporting Cells and a small handful were adapted briefly as RGHQs and for other civil contingency purposes.

Many public utilities built protected emergency control rooms and other facilities as elements of what, in modern parlance, would be called business continuity programmes. The most comprehensively equipped of these organisations was the telephone arm of the General Post Office, the publicly owned forerunner of British Telecom. Although the GPO provided domestic and business telephone services to the country at large, during the 1950s and early 1960s its primary function was the provision of essential communication services to the government and armed services. For many years almost its entire budget was devoted to defence purposes, including the laying of tens of thousands of miles of new cables to link Royal Observer Corps sites into the Rotor network and to provide cabling and equipment to handle the vast amounts of data and landline voice transmissions generated by the decentralised nature of the new radar system.

During the aftermath of a nuclear attack a reliable emergency communications system would be the paramount requirement to ensure any semblance of continuity of government. This could be provided only by the GPO landline cable network, with long distance communications carried, along with all the radar and other defence traffic, over existing underground trunk lines on the public network. The problem was that these trunk lines tended to pass through city centre exchanges, which in the peacetime civilian world made commercial sense, but in wartime rendered them highly vulnerable. To counter this threat in the cities assessed as most vulnerable of all – London, Birmingham and Manchester – trunk cables were carried in ducts over one hundred feet below ground and, beneath the city centres, huge emergency telephone exchanges were constructed at a similar depth. The *Anchor* exchange beneath Birmingham, and Manchester's *Guardian* exchange, were constructed in newly excavated tunnels but in London advantage was taken of an existing deep-level air-raid shelter beneath Chancery Lane tube station. London clay is an exceptionally easy material to tunnel through, so lots of tunnels have been dug through it and, not infrequently, have remained unused after completion. During the Second World War the Ministry of Home Security constructed a series of deep-level bomb shelters on alignments beneath the Central and Northern lines on the tacit understanding that after the war they would be integrated into proposed new high-speed north-south and east-west rail links. The deep-level shelter at Chancery Lane, which was on the east-west Central Line alignment, was never used as a shelter during the war and, in the post-war years, London Transport was unwilling to proceed with construction of either of the high-speed lines. The GPO, however, bit the bullet, considerably extended the existing tunnels and there established the enormous *Kingsway* underground trunk exchange.

During the 1950s strategic GPO trunk cable routes were deviated around other major cities and, close to these cities, and at other key locations, eight fallout-protected, semi-underground repeater

stations were built. Each was provided with air filtration equipment, standby generators and fuel and water supplies sufficient for them to operate for four weeks under 'close-down' conditions. Smaller, rather anonymous, radiation-protected repeater stations were built in numerous locations throughout the country but records are sparse and their locations are only slowly being identified. At many larger conventional exchanges piles of interlocking bricks with a high lead content were provided with which staff would be expected, in event of an emergency, to build their own fallout shelter upon a template painted on a basement floor.

Probably the most numerous of the utility bunkers were those constructed by the various water boards or their successor water companies. Located mainly at remote waterworks sites (although Severn Trent Water's principal bunker was beneath their new office complex near Gloucester), most were built towards the end of the Cold War and many remained unfinished.

Almost all of these bunkers are now abandoned. Some have been demolished, either quickly and purposefully because they offered ripe development potential, or else more slowly in a piecemeal fashion at the hands of vandals and arsonists. Many others are being slowly reclaimed by nature while others still, in rural areas, have found more ignominious uses as cow sheds or rough storage for agricultural implements. At a disconcertingly large number of sites, the underground bunkers seem to have been inundated by seepage water almost immediately after the doors were closed for the last time. A few structures have found new and often commercially sensitive uses as high security storage facilities or data centres and are omitted from this book at their owners' request.

The threat of a nuclear strike on the UK by the Eastern Bloc, which drove the construction of these underground refuges and command posts, has long since faded. The deterrence of mutual assured destruction ('MAD') meant that none of the structures, services and systems were ever used in anger. The Cold War was a virtual war, with no battles and few victims; a war, arguably, with only victors and no losers. As such, there are no memorials in the conventional sense to the more than 40 years of preparation for what never came. But the bunkers in this book themselves stand as monuments to this period and to the provision of what may, in the final analysis, have offered no more than a ringside seat for the complete annihilation of the United Kingdom.

Chapter 2

REGIONAL WAR ROOMS

Planning for the Regional War Rooms was initiated in October 1951. Their design was based upon the Civil Defence experience of the Second World War and it was expected that their administrative functions in any future war would be broadly similar. From here, the rescue effort would be organised and the supply of essential services co-ordinated.

At the time of their construction the greatest risk was perceived as blast, so the buildings were made immensely strong with reinforced concrete walls four feet ten inches thick and roofs five feet thick.

For administrative purposes the country was divided into twelve regions, each of which was provided with a War Room. Additional to this number, London was divided into four quadrants and each of these was allocated its own War Room.

All the provincial War Rooms were new, two-storey structures built to one of two standard designs – either semi-underground or constructed entirely above ground level – except for the example at Newcastle upon Tyne where the existing, Second World War RAF No.13 Group Operations Room at Kenton Bar was adapted.

Below: The long disused Bristol War Room, located at the Flowers Hill Government Estate in Brislington, almost engulfed in Virginia creeper.

Brislington

Left: Interior of the central control cabin on the lower floor of the bunker, looking out into the map room.

Below left: The telephone communications room. The upright projections above the dividers between each cubicle are message clips. Message forms completed by the telephone operators would be placed here for collection by messengers who would deliver them by hand to the relevant offices.

Below right: This curious device, made by the Lamson Company (more famous for its pneumatic tube systems), was used to transfer small packages of messages between the upper and lower floor of the bunker.

Opposite: By 1982 the bunker was in possession of Bristol City Council. In that year they rather grudgingly participated in the nation-wide Home Office 'Square Leg' civil defence exercise. After completion of the exercise the bunker was abandoned with all the 'Square Leg' paraphernalia still in place.

Right: Brislington's standby diesel generator in its supposedly sound-proof enclosure on the lower floor of the bunker.

Below: The ventilation fan in the lower floor plant room. External air was drawn in through banks of filters via large concrete ducts on the roof of the bunker. In certain circumstances the plant could be temporarily changed over to a recirculatory mode which excluded the ingress of contaminated external air.

Opposite right: The control room in the Cheadle War Room, seen here in its final role as the Greater Manchester Emergency Centre.

Opposite left: A manual telephone exchange in the communications centre at Cheadle.

Cheadle

Above: Following its closure in 1958 the Cheadle War Room functioned as a Sub-Regional Control until 1964 when it became the Manchester Corporation main Civil Defence Control. Decommissioned in 1968, it was reactivated from 1981 until 1991 as the Greater Manchester Emergency Centre. The bunker was demolished in 2002.

Above: Ventilation ducts on the roof of the Coryton War Room.

Below: These bunk beds date from the latter period of the bunker's life when it functioned as the South Glamorgan Emergency Centre.

Coryton

Above: Following its decommissioning in 1958 the Coryton bunker functioned until 1968 as the Cardiff Corporation Civil Defence Control. Between 1974 and its final abandonment in 1991 it was the South Glamorgan Emergency Centre. The bunker was demolished in 2005.

Below: The kitchen. Similar facilities existed in all the Regional War Rooms.

Above: The operations room at Coryton.

Leeds

Left: Following its closure in 1958 the Leeds War Room, situated on the Lawnswood Government Estate, functioned in the dual role of a Sub-Control of the York Regional Seat of Government and as Leeds City Council Civil Defence control centre.

Following the 1968 Civil Defence cutbacks the bunker fell into disuse until 1981 when it was half-heartedly refurbished as the Leeds City Emergency Control. By that time, however, the lower areas were subject to flooding and the upper floor – all that was tenable – was used only sporadically. It has now been long disused but remains in reasonable external condition.

Below: The flooded lower level. Surprisingly, the top floor remained in use for some years after water began to rise in the lower floor map room.

Below: The main ventilation fan in the plant room. The brick chamber beyond contains air filters, accessible for cleaning via the hatch on the side.

Tunbridge Wells

Above: After a period of disuse following the abandonment of the Regional War Rooms, the Tunbridge Wells bunker became home to the first incarnation of the Police National Computer (PNC). Several years of use as a secure document store followed, until the bunker was finally demolished in 1997.

Below left: Although little is recorded of this period, it is probable that the Police National Computer was housed in this room.

Below right: The kitchen in the Tunbridge Wells bunker.

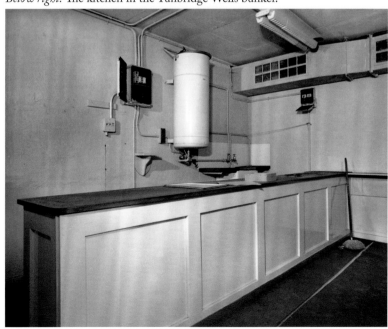

Shirley

Above right: The Birmingham War Room, situated on Stratford Road in Shirley, lay abandoned for many years following decommissioning in 1958. The bunker served as Birmingham Corporation's main Civil Defence control from 1965 until 1968. It was acquired by British Gas during the 1970s and used by that company and its successor, Transco, as a document archive until 2000. It was demolished the following year.

Reading

Above left: The function of the Reading War Room at Whiteknights Park was usurped in 1958 by a newly established RSG at nearby Warren Row. The latter was built in a chalk mine which had been converted into an underground factory during the Second World War. Briefly, the War Room acted as a communications centre for Warren Row but in more recent years has been utilized as document repository by Reading University Library.

Left: The remote indicator dials above the generator cubicle door are a minor but unusual feature of the Reading War Room.

Kenton Bar

The Newcastle Regional War Room at Kenton Bar is unique in that it is the only War Room to have been built within an existing structure. The original bunker was constructed in 1939 and commissioned in March 1940 as the Operations Room for No.13 Group, RAF Fighter Command.

After decommissioning in 1945, a number of post-war uses were proposed for the bunker, including conversion to the Northern Sector Operations Centre for the Rotor radar system. This, however, did not come to fruition and instead it took on the role of Regional War Room.

Left: The surface entrance building.

Below left: The stairwell into the underground bunker.

Below: Ventilation equipment in the underground plant room.

Above: The map room in the Kenton Bar War Room was formerly the Operations Room of No.13 Group RAF Fighter Command and is quite unlike any other Regional War Room or RAF Group Headquarters. The rectangular Fresnel light fittings on the ceiling are original and date from the bunker's RAF origins; the relatively modern spotlight fittings may date from the late 1960s when it was used as an occasional training centre for RSG staff. In the 1970s it was proposed as a possible location for the Tyne and Wear County War Headquarters but nothing came of this. It is currently disused.

Restoration of the bunker began in 2009, with the aim of eventually opening it to the public.

LONDON WAR ROOMS

Under the original scheme London was designated as Region No.5 and would have four separate bunkers – one serving each quadrant of the city – located at Cheam, Chiselhurst, Mill Hill and Wanstead. Similar in outward appearance to the provincial bunkers, the London War Rooms were surface structures on only one level. When the scheme was abandoned in 1958 Region No.5 ceased to exist and London would have been jointly controlled by the four surrounding Regional Seats of Government. In 1965 Region No.5 was revived, with its control in the former Rotor Sector Operations Centre at Kelvedon Hatch.

Cheam
Above: In later years the former Cheam War Room was used as Sutton Borough Control. The building has now been demolished.

Chiselhurst
Left: The Chiselhurst War Room was abandoned in 1958 and lay derelict for decades.
Below left and right: In recent years it has been converted at enormous expense into a spectacular private residence. These photographs of the conversion in progress show the remarkable thickness of the walls and roof.

Mill Hill

Above and below: After 1958 it was suggested that the Mill Hill War Room should become Barnet Council's emergency centre, but little came of the scheme. Abandoned for many years, the bunker was listed Grade II in 2002 but, despite this, it was radically converted into a private dwelling in 2010.

Pear Tree House

The bunker at Pear Tree House in Lambeth's Central Hill Estate was built in 1966 and occupies the basement of a block of eight two-bedroomed flats. The main entrance is by way of a steel blast-door at lower-ground-level with an emergency exit accessed from an external stairway. Initially planned as a London Group Control, it was demoted to Lambeth Borough Control before construction was completed.

With the end of Civil Defence in 1968 the bunker was placed under care and maintenance. In 1973 the Greater London Council divided the city into five groups for emergency planning purposes, each with its own control centre. This was a slow business but, in 1977, Pear Tree House was designated as the South East Group War Headquarters.

During the 1980s the bunker attracted much attention from the media and anti-nuclear organizations such as CND. Amid much political turmoil – Lambeth declared itself a Nuclear Free Zone – it seemed probable that funding would be withdrawn and the bunker would be closed. Compromises were made, however, and the site continued in use until its final closure in 1993.

Opposite: The main operations room and communications centre are on the lower floor of the bunker with generator and electrical switchgear in the extension below the external staircase. The upper floor of the bunker contains welfare facilities, dormitories and administrative offices.

Below: The operations room in January 2001, littered with paperwork from the last days of the Cold War.

Wanstead

Above: In 1971 the Wanstead War Room assumed the role of Redbridge Borough control. The folding bunks *(left)* and the main operations room *(below)* date from this period. The bunker was demolished in 2000.

Southall

Above: This site was originally planned as a new town hall for Southall but only the basement was built. The vault doors visible in this picture were intended to be the town hall strong-rooms. The basement was used as the control for Southall Urban District Council during the Second World War and continued to fulfil this function until 1965 It then became the control for the new London Borough of Ealing. It remained their control until 1991 but

was not maintained after 1968. From 1951 to 1957 it was a Sub-Divisional control for Middlesex and, from 1977, was designated as the GLC North West Control, but no progress was made with the plan at that time (flood emergencies for the GLC North West area were dealt with at the Hillingdon Council bunker). A full upgrade was proposed in 1991, by which time it was under the control of the London Fire and Civil Defence Authority, the successor to the GLC. The end of the Cold War led to the abandonment of this scheme. Hanborough Junior School has now been built over the bunker.

Glasgow

Above: The War Room on the site of the Scottish National Engineering Laboratory Technology Park at East Kilbride was originally intended to function as the Western Regional Sub-Control under the main Scottish War Room at Kirknewton. A similar Eastern Region Sub-Control planned for Livingston was never built. The East Kilbride War Room, pictured above, is a single-storey structure identical to the four London War Rooms. In the early 1960s its function was transferred to the former Anti-Aircraft Operations Room at Torrance House and for a while the East Kilbride bunker was relegated to a Civil Defence Group Control for the Glasgow area. Closed down in 1968, it was reactivated in 1974 as Strathclyde County Control. With the end of the Cold War, it was finally decommissioned in 1996. The bunker is now Grade C listed by Historic Scotland.

WAR ROOMS ADAPTED AS REGIONAL SEATS OF GOVERNMENT

Kirknewton

Below: The availability of many redundant Rotor radar bunkers in the late 1950s facilitated a major revamp of the emergency regional structure in Scotland. In 1965 Scotland was divided into three zones with the Northern Zone Control located in the former Rotor bunker at Anstruther, the Western Zone Control in the former Anti-Aircraft Operations Room at Torrance House and the Eastern Zone Control in the former Scottish Regional War Room at Kirknewton. The Scottish Central Control was established in the redundant Rotor Sector Operations Centre at Barnton Quarry near Edinburgh in 1962. In 1964 the large two-storey extension with prominent air intakes on the roof, visible in the photograph below, was constructed to house the much enlarged staff at Kirknewton when the bunker took over the role of Central Control from Barnton Quarry. Control reverted to Barnton Quarry around 1980, at which time Kirknewton became a combined control for the Central and Eastern regions.

The bunker was finally closed in 1990 when it was replaced by a purpose-built RGHQ at Cultybraggan. It was used for a number of generally unsuccessful commercial purposes, including a night club, before it was eventually demolished in August 2003.

Above left: The standby generator in the new plant room in the extension built in the mid-1960s.

Above: Much of the communications equipment, like this five position manual switchboard, remained in the bunker and survived in various states of dilapidation until its demolition.

Left: During the 1990s part of the bunker was occupied by the Scottish Office who conducted some bizarre experiments there. In the two-storey central map room they experimented with various explosive devices; the empty, blackened, windowless and doorless shell seen here is the result.

Cambridge

Above: The Cambridge Regional War Room, situated in a Government Estate at Brooklands Avenue, was extended in 1963 for use as the Regional Seat of Government for No.4 Region. The two-storey extension effectively tripled the size of the bunker, increasing its staff capacity from fifty to over two hundred. Following a period of apparent disuse a programme of refurbishment was started in 1990 to prepare the bunker as an Armed Forces Headquarters for No.4 Region. This work was overtaken by the end of the Cold War and was never completed.

Standby diesel power plants in the original War Room *(above)*, and in the RSG extension *(below)*. The diesel generator shown below was probably installed during the 1990 refurbishment.

Above: Ventilation fan and filter chamber in the original War Room.

Below: Part of the air-conditioning equipment in the new plant room.

Left: A corner of the extended kitchen in the 1965 extension.

Below left: The BBC studio, left unfinished in 1990 when the proposed upgrade to the status of Sub-Control to the new RGHQ at Bawburgh was abandoned.

Below right: In the original War Room a floor was inserted in the double-height map room. The original curved windows can be seen in this view of the new upper-floor conference room.

Nottingham

Above: The Regional War Room at Chalfont Drive in Nottingham underwent a radical transformation in 1963 to convert it into the Regional Seat of Government for No.3 Region. A two-storey extension was added to one end of the structure and a third level, spanning the whole length of the original building with wide cantilevered extensions supported by external concrete pillars, was added to the top of the structure.

The bunker served as a Regional Seat of Government for only a few years and was handed over in 1969 to the Ministry of Agriculture, Fisheries and Food. When visited in 2002, parts of the building were used to store MAFF paraphernalia including foot and mouth disease warning signs. Most of the lower floor was filled with countless thousands of old Ordnance Survey plans dumped there by the Land Registry. The bunker is now listed Grade II by English Heritage.

Left: Air-conditioning plant in the extended plant room.

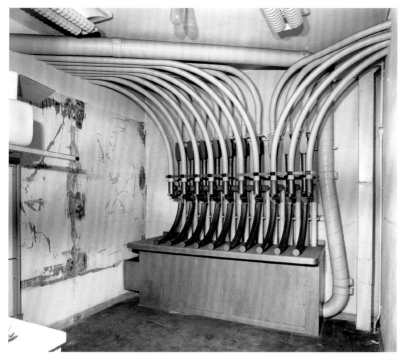

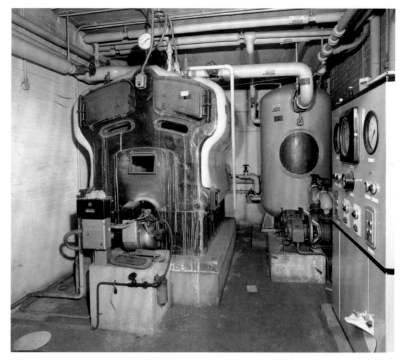

Above: The pneumatic Lamson Tube exchange, installed during the conversion to a Regional Seat of Government in 1963. Using this system original documents could be transferred between offices in small cylinders propelled through pipes by air pressure.

Below: The large new kitchen and servery constructed in the RSG extension. The original kitchen in the old Regional War Room was also retained.

Above: The oil-fired central heating boiler and heat exchanger in the bunker's plant room.

Below: The BBC studio, lined with acoustic panelling.

Chapter 3

REGIONAL GOVERNMENT HEADQUARTERS

Ballymena

Below: Plans for the complete overhaul of the Civil Defence organization in Northern Ireland were proposed in 1985. Central to these plans was the construction of a state-of-the-art RGHQ bunker at Ballymena in County Antrim. The design would be similar to a series of new RGHQs currently under construction at various locations on the British mainland, notably at Chilmark in Wiltshire and Cultybraggan in Stirlingshire.

The bunker is of two-storey semi-underground construction. The lower floor is completely underground and the upper floor is protected by a substantial earth mound. The most prominent feature of the bunker is the array of concrete ventilation towers that rise from the top of the mound.

The lower floor houses the standby generators, air-conditioning plant and the most important of the government offices. The upper floor is dedicated primarily to welfare services and includes kitchen and dining facilities, dormitories for the two-hundred-strong staff, as well as a range of administrative offices. Construction of the bunker began in 1987 and was completed in 1990.

Left: Two standby generators, painted a startling shade of blue, in the lower floor plant room.

Bottom left: Bunk beds in one of the upper-floor dormitories. Although finished to a high standard it is obvious that space here was at a premium.

Bottom right: Part of the ventilation system in the lower-floor plant room showing four induction fans with a bank of air filters to the right.

Left: A typical view showing the high standard of finish in the bunker's administrative office space.

Left: The servery in the bunker's restaurant area. All the RGHQs constructed or refurbished in the late 1980s were provided with very high quality catering facilities.

Above: Interior view of the guardroom and security centre.

Below left and right: The BBC broadcasting studio and control room.

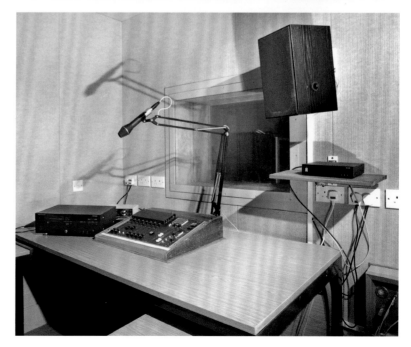

Bridgend

Above and right: The bunker at Bridgend started life in the early 1960s as one of two Sub-Regional Headquarters for Wales. A suitable location for the second headquarters in North Wales was never found so the whole load devolved upon Bridgend. The bunker is situated on the site of the former Brackla Royal Ordnance Factory and was constructed within a pair of adjacent underground high-explosives magazines that served the factory.

Each magazine consisted of two parallel 250-feet-long iron-lined tunnels approximately fifty feet apart, connected laterally by eight large storage chambers. Each magazine was served by a standard-gauge railway line and an underground loading platform. The storage chambers and loading platforms were adapted to provide the necessary office space for the SRHQ. New extensions were built to house air-conditioning plant on the upper floor and generators on the lower floor.

The two bunkers, which are virtually independent, are connected underground by a 250 foot long pedestrian tunnel.

The site was extensively refurbished in the late 1980s to become the RGHQ for Wales. It was decommissioned and sold a few years later in 1995.

Above: The somewhat sinister outline of the Chilmark ventilation towers provides a surreal backdrop to the valley of the river Nadder in Wiltshire.

Chilmark

Home Office plans for the development of a new RGHQ at Chilmark – intended to replace the existing and hopelessly inefficient Sub-Regional Control at Ullenwood near Gloucester – were initiated in the early 1980s. Working drawings were prepared towards the end of 1982 and within three years construction was well under way. Both of the bunkers which it replaced were adaptations of buildings erected in the early 1950s, the former as a GCI station in the Rotor radar scheme and the latter as an Anti-Aircraft Operations Room.

The two-level bunker, which is approximately 200 feet in length and some forty feet wide, is located on gently sloping ground overlooking the Nadder Valley at Ham Cross near Chilmark and is adjacent to the rail interchange sidings of an extensive, former RAF underground bomb store. The Home Office bunker did not take advantage of the existing disused subterranean quarry workings in the area, but the proximity of a significant military site,

and the ramifications of this presence in terms of external ground defence, probably influenced its location.

The building was constructed on a rock plateau excavated into the hillside and, when completed, was covered with earth to a minimum depth of ten feet. External walls are of two-feet-thick reinforced concrete. Little is evident above ground other than a series of prominent ventilation stacks on the hilltop above the bunker, and a pair of inclined entrance shafts into the hillside. Within the structure the lower floor is dedicated to office accommodation and operational areas. The upper floor, which is marginally less well protected against blast and heat, contains the headquarters' dormitories and welfare facilities, although there are also some administrative area there. Almost one third of the bunker is given over to service installations such as standby generators, power distribution cubicles and air-conditioning plant.

Left: A section of the suite of offices provided for the Regional Commissioner's secretariat. The typical 1980s décor, and the quality of the fitting-out, is clearly evident in this photograph. Compare this with the sparseness of the equivalent Regional War Rooms of the 1950s or the Regional Seats of Government of the subsequent decades.

Below: Corridor of power: the central spine corridor on the lower level of the bunker. Excluding the service area, this passage runs the full length of the building and terminates at stairwells at each end. The door to the immediate left is to the military communication suite, the first room on the right housed the uniformed services and is followed by the secretariat offices, the BBC studio and the strong-room.

Above: The servery in the headquarters' restaurant. The high standard of fixtures and fittings within the bunker is evident here too. Note the stainless steel fittings (including refrigerators and deep freezers in the background) and the tastefully tiled floor.

Above: The principal entrance to the bunker, with the ventilation towers on the hillside above. The left-hand incline gives access to the service areas on the lower level, including the generators and air-conditioning plant. The right-hand incline accesses the main administrative areas of the bunker. Both entrance portals give onto narrow, dog-leg corridors terminating in massive steel blast doors that secure the main body of the bunker.

Left: The generator room on the lower floor of the self-contained service area of the bunker. Each of the two generators is capable of sustaining the normal load of the establishment under emergency working conditions. The second unit is a standby in case of a failure of the main plant.

Left: The central electricity distribution room. From here power is distributed throughout the bunker for lighting, heating and ventilation purposes. Switchgear is also provided to control the air-conditioning plant situated on the floor above. Power is normally taken from the national grid but in the event of a grid failure then the main generator would switch in automatically. The internal power plant could also be switched in manually from this point, or remotely simply by pressing a single prominent button in the guard room near the bunker's main pedestrian entrance.

Above: The new upper floor entrance to the Crowborough RGHQ with the prominent ventilation towers to the left.

Crowborough

The RGHQ at Crowborough in East Sussex was built within the shell of the underground wartime Political Warfare Executive wireless propaganda transmitter station known as *Aspidistra*. The bunker was constructed in 1942 and at the end of hostilities was retained by the Foreign Office for use by the Diplomatic Wireless Service during the post-war years. For some years the

BBC broadcast World Service programmes using the *Aspidistra* transmitter.

Acquired by the Home Office, the bunker was completely rebuilt, a new mezzanine floor inserted, new entrances made, and a new plant room extension constructed between 1984 and 1986, in order to replace the earlier and highly unsuitable *Dumpy* bunker below Dover Castle. The bunker stands within the secure boundary of the Sussex Police training centre.

Above and below: Although the catering facilities at Crowborough were built on a smaller scale than those at the other 1980s period RGHQs they were still fitted out to a remarkably high standard.

Above: The original, gently-inclined *Aspidistra* entrance tunnel – just about all that survives of the original structure.
Below: Blast doors securing the upper-floor main entrance.

Reconstruction of the *Aspidistra* bunker included the addition of an intermediate third floor, made possible by the existence of deep cable ducts beneath the original floor levels.

The upper floor contained catering and domestic facilities, the middle floor the principal administrative offices, and the lower floor a BBC studio, engineering services and senior staff accommodation.

A new upper-floor wing was added to provide space for air-conditioning equipment, standby generators and other service plant.

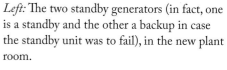

Left: The two standby generators (in fact, one is a standby and the other a backup in case the standby unit was to fail), in the new plant room.

Left: Part of the complex air-conditioning and ventilation equipment also enclosed within the new plant room extension.

Cultybraggan

Above: The Scottish RGHQ at Cultybraggan near Stirling was one of the small number of purpose-built emergency headquarters constructed in the 1980s. All were broadly similar in design with two floors, the lower floor completely buried and the upper floor protected by an earth mound.

The Cultybraggan bunker replaced an earlier SRHQ at Anstruther which had been constructed in a converted underground Rotor GCI operations room.

The bunker, which is situated within an Army training range, was commissioned in 1990 but closed down two years later at the end of the Cold War and transferred to Army control. Cultybraggan Camp, which includes the bunker, was purchased by the Comrie Development Trust in 2007.

Left: An extensive bank of air-filters in the bunker's ventilation plant.

Above and below: The BBC broadcasting and control rooms.

Above: An SX2000 message switching cubical linked to the Emergency Communications Network (ECN) in the BT equipment room.
Below: Medical facilities in the bunker's sick bay.

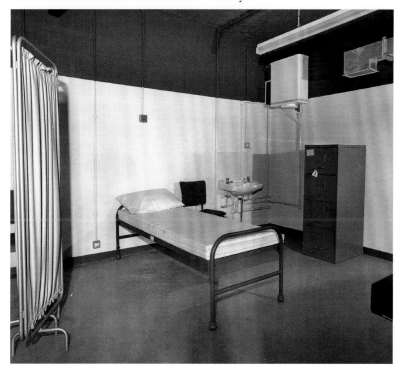

Drakelow

Above: An extensive network of tunnels was excavated between 1941 and 1943 in the sandstone hills at Drakelow, near Kidderminster, in which to construct a secure underground aircraft engine factory.

In 1958 the then redundant tunnels were acquired by the Home Office and a section that formerly housed the factory's offices, storage areas and welfare facilities was converted into a Regional Seat of Government (RSG-9), serving the West Midlands Region. During the 1980s the bunker was completely refurbished and physically reduced in scale to become the West Midlands RGHQ. The bunker was finally decommissioned in 1993.

Many of the earlier RSG facilities including the kitchens and BBC broadcasting studio were not included in the refurbishment and still survive, in a state of considerable disrepair, in abandoned sections of the tunnels.

Occasional public visits were organised through the local Tourist Information Centre, but there stopped in 2009 due to damage caused by an airsoft group that made use of the tunnels.

Above: The abandoned kitchen of the former Regional Seat of Government at Drakelow. This probably included fixtures from the wartime factory kitchen.
Below: A corner of the new catering facilities provided at the Drakelow RGHQ at the time of the 1980s refit.

Above: The derelict remains of the earlier BBC broadcasting studio in the abandoned RSG.
Below: A view of the replacement BBC studio constructed in the 1980s to serve the upgraded RGHQ.

'Dumpy' – Dover Castle

Above: In 1941 a new series of tunnels was dug in the chalk cliffs beneath the Napoleonic tunnels under Dover Castle to serve as a Joint Services Headquarters for forces guarding the Northern Channel. The tunnels were abandoned until 1962 when they were taken over by the Home Office for conversion into a Regional Seat of Government (RSG-12). This view shows the Tape Relay Centre within the bunker's Signals Centre.

Although Dumpy is located below Hellfire Corner at Dover Castle, which is a popular tourist attraction, the tunnels are considered unsafe and no public access is allowed.

Above: The generator room at *Dumpy* after the removal of the diesel generators. Note the exhaust silencers in the roof of the tunnel.
Below: Air-conditioning ducting in the plant room in the Dover tunnels.

Above: An access tunnel in the *Dumpy* bunker with a passenger lift to the left and office accommodation ahead.
Below: A typical access corridor within *Dumpy*.

Above: The entrance to the southern bunker at Swynnerton showing the extension (painted green) built to house the powerhouse and air-conditioning plant.

Swynnerton

Like the Welsh RGHQ at Bridgend, RGHQ 9.1 at Swynnerton in Staffordshire was constructed in a pair of adjacent underground explosives magazines at a former Royal Ordnance Factory. At the time of conversion a new underground concrete walkway was built to connect the two bunkers.

It would appear that the site was first adapted as a Civil Defence Control by North Staffordshire Council but was abandoned in 1968 following the winding up of the Civil Defence organization.

The bunker was reactivated in the late 1970s as a SRHQ and substantially rebuilt and refitted in 1988 to serve as a Regional Government Headquarters. The refit included the construction of new two-storey extensions at the entrance to each of the bunkers to house the upgraded air-conditioning plants, generators and switchgear.

Above and below: Although the catering facilities at all the new RGHQs built in the 1980s were provided to a uniformly high standard, they were not, as can be seen from these photographs, built to a standard design.

Above: Circulating pumps installed to provide adequate pressures of domestic and process water throughout the combined bunkers.

Below: Water supplies sufficient for fourteen days stored within the bunker.

Chapter 4

THE ROTOR RADAR SYSTEM

Above: Guard houses at all the Rotor stations were built to a standard design with slight variations to incorporate local building materials. At all the stations with underground operations bunkers, like this Sector Operations Centre at Bawburgh, underground access was via a stairwell in an extension attached to the rear of the guardroom. The bunkers were joined to the stairwells by long underground corridors, protected by blast doors.

The abandonment of most of Britain's wartime radar defences in the late 1940s left the country dangerously vulnerable just as the Soviet Union appeared to seriously threaten national security. The Rotor programme, initiated in 1950, was designed to restore full radar coverage to the whole Main Defended Area (MDA) of the United Kingdom around the east and south coasts from Flamborough Head to Portland Bill. Initially, twelve existing Chain Home (CH)

stations would be refurbished, followed by four Chain Home Extra Low (CHEL) stations and six Centimetric Early Warning (CEW) stations along the east and southeast coasts. The CHEL stations were low level radars capable of detecting aircraft flying below the range of the CH stations. CEW stations employed a more advanced high frequency radar that was effective from ground level to high altitudes.

It was hoped that by September 1953 eleven Ground Control Intercept (GCI) stations would be completed along the coast of the MDA and that by late 1953 a further fourteen GCI stations would be completed in the Midlands and the West Country. All the east and south coast stations would be provided with underground control rooms while GCI stations situated further west would have blast-protected semi-underground control bunkers.

Financial constraints led to the later GCI control centres being of inexpensive prefabricated construction with no blast protection. Some, including Charmy Down, were only partially completed when the whole system was rendered obsolete by the development of ballistic missiles.

Under the original plan the country was divided into six air-defence sectors each provided with a central Sector Operations Centre (SOC) to which surveillance radars in its sector would report. Based upon these reports the SOC would issue warnings to the sector GCI stations which would alert its fighter airfields accordingly. Following the introduction of Type 80 radars, however, the SOCs were rendered prematurely redundant.

The final phase of Rotor envisaged the scheme extended to cover northwest Scotland and the Western Approaches, but technological developments elsewhere overtook it before it was fully implemented.

Installation of the electronic apparatus was intended to be done on a progressive basis as new equipment currently under development came into production. This scheme was, however, upset, as we have seen in the introduction, by the surprisingly rapid evolution of the Type 80 radar. Implementation of Type 80 necessitated a number of design alterations within the stations, including the construction of deep wells below each plotting room to house Kelvin Hughes photographic projectors in place of manual plotting tables, and the construction of separate radar-modulator buildings. The latter contained high-power electronic equipment to produce the constantly changing operational frequencies that made Type 80 difficult to jam.

The Rotor control bunkers were built to a series of standard designs, each prefixed 'R':

R1 - single-storey underground	CEW
R2 - single-storey underground	CHEL
R3 - two-storey underground	GCI
R4 - three-storey	SOC
R5 - design abandoned	
R6 - two-storey semi-underground	GCI
R7 - underground remote well for type 7 radar head	

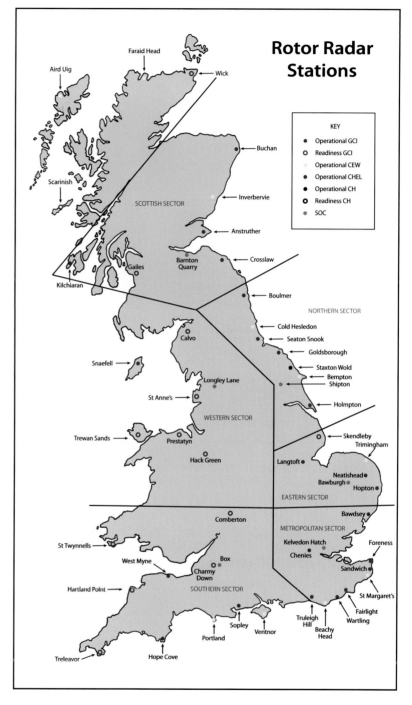

Rotor Radar Stations

KEY
- ● Operational GCI
- ○ Readiness GCI
- · Operational CEW
- ● Operational CHEL
- ● Operational CH
- ○ Readiness CH
- · SOC

R8 - single-storey prefabricated surface building	GCI
R9 - proposed conversion of 'Happidrome' (not implemented)	
R10 - single-storey surface building	CEW
R11 - single-storey surface building	CHEL

TYPE R4 SECTOR OPERATIONS CENTRES

Barnton Quarry

Above: Barnton Quarry is on the outskirts of Edinburgh and during the Second World War was home to an RAF Fighter Command Operations Room. This structure still survives, although in very poor condition.

In 1952, on a site immediately adjacent to the Sector Operations Room, work began on the construction of a three-level Rotor Sector Operations Centre which would control radar surveillance and interception within the Caledonian area.

By 1958 the Sector Operations Centres were redundant and a few years later, in the early 1960s, the Barnton Quarry bunker was transformed into a Regional Seat of Government for Scotland. The emergency government scheme for Scotland was in a state of constant flux and over the next decade or so the bunker assumed a variety of roles. In 1984 the site, by now disused, was acquired by Lothian Council which sold it three years later to a property developer. The site remained unused and changed hands again in 1992 but before any commercial development could be started the interior of the bunker was completely destroyed by fire – probably the result of vandalism – and the subsequent asbestos contamination has put a question mark over the site's future.

Right: One of the air-conditioning compressors, stripped for scrap metal.

Opposite: The remains of the central operations room completely gutted by fire in the early 1990s.

Above: The vandalised remains of electro-mechanical switchgear in the telecommunications room.
Below: The systematic theft of scrap metal is evident in this photograph.

Above: Wrecked switchgear in the air-conditioning plant room.
Below: Another view showing the extent of the damage in the air-conditioning plant room.

Box Wiltshire

During the mid-1930s large tracts of disused underground stone quarries in the Corsham area of North Wiltshire were taken over by the War Office and converted into ammunition depots.

In 1940 a small quarry heading known as Brown's Quarry, immediately adjacent to Tunnel Quarry (the largest of the War Office ammunition depots), was acquired by the RAF and converted into an underground operations room for No.10 Group, Fighter Command, known as RAF Box.

No.10 Group was disbanded at the end of the war but the operations room continued in use for a number of years in various radar training roles. In 1952, as an economy measure, it was decided to adapt the existing underground structure as the Southern Sector Operations Centre under the Rotor programme rather than provide a purpose-built R4 bunker. Brown's Quarry was for some time also the Southern Sector Headquarters for UKWMO.

Following the demise of the Rotor Sector Operations Centres in 1958 the operations room at RAF Box was abandoned. By the mid-1970s the timber mezzanine floors were suffering serious decay and were all removed as a safety measure.

Below: The entrance to the UKWMO Sector Operations Centre which was co-located with the Rotor SOC at Box.

Above and below: Two views of the underground operations room at Box, after removal of the timber balconies. Note the large steel girders supporting the quarry roof.

Kelvedon Hatch

The three-level R4 Sector Operations Room at Kelvedon Hatch in Essex was established in 1953 to co-ordinate surveillance and interception by radar stations in the Metropolitan Sector of the Rotor radar system. Like all the other SOCs, Kelvedon Hatch was rendered obsolete by 1958.

Between 1964 and 1968 the bunker was converted into a Home Office Sub-Regional Control with responsibility for the London region.

In 1993 the site was sold back to the landowners from whom it was compulsorily purchased in the 1950s and is now open to the public as a Cold War museum.

Above right and left: The guard house and underground access corridor to the bunker.

Right: Part of the bunker's air-conditioning plant room.

Shipton

The Northern Sector R4 Operations Centre at Shipton in North Yorkshire was closed down in 1958 but was refurbished in the early 1960s for a new role in the Home Office emergency regional government scheme. In the early 1980s the site underwent a major reconstruction – including the addition of a new upper floor to provide dormitories and additional plant accommodation - to prepare it for its new role as an RGHQ. This did not last long, however, as the bunker was closed down and stripped of its fittings in 1993.

Above: The anonymous looking guard house at Shipton.

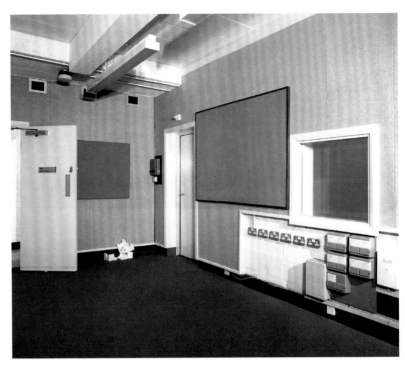

Above: The BBC studio at Shipton, added when the bunker was extended and refurbished as a RGHQ.

Below: A view along the main underground access corridor looking towards the stairwell.

Below: A view down the main stairwell between floors in the bunker.

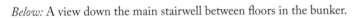

TYPE R1 CEW STATIONS

Beachy Head

The Rotor station at Beachy Head was opened in December 1952 . Initially it was provided with two Type 13 and two Type 14 surveillance radars, supplemented soon after, as an interim measure, with an American AN/FPS3 unit. In 1954 an advanced Type 80 radar was installed. Within three years the site was redundant and was placed on care and maintenance in 1957.

Following its permanent closure in 1960 the local authority made an unsuccessful approach to acquire the bunker for use as a Civil Defence control. Over the subsequent decades the bunker has been badly vandalised and is now sealed. The guardhouse, which had been used by the coastguard, has now been demolished.

Right: The remains of the operations room in the mid-1980s.

Below left: The bunker's primary air filtration plant in the background with the remains of a gas filtration unit in the foreground.

Below right: A view towards the emergency exit staircase with the air filters visible to the left.

Above: The plotting room at Bempton, showing the well which once contained the Kelvin-Hughes projector. Note the ventilation ducts and service connections still in place.

Bempton

Above: Like at so many of the Rotor stations, both the above and below ground features have suffered extensive vandalism.

Right: The badly vandalised operations room at Bempton.

Below: This structure served a dual function as a ventilation shaft and emergency exit for the underground bunker.

Inverbervie

Following the demise of Rotor the CEW station at Inverbervie came under the control of RAF Edzel and was involved with the US Navy Oceanographic Monitoring Organization. In 1985 the bunker became the Emergency Armed Forces Headquarters for the Grampian and Tayside region, until its closure in 1993. The site was finally sold in 1999 and the guard house converted into a private residence. The photographs on this page show the bunker in its final incarnation as an Armed Forces Headquarters.

Above left: The two-level control room at Inverbervie. The alterations to the balcony were probably made while the US Navy Oceanographic Monitoring Organization was in residence.

Above right: This three-position manual telephone switchboard in the bunker's communication centre dates from the time that it served as an Emergency Armed Forces Headquarters.

Left: The air-conditioning plant-room, unchanged from the time of its installation in the early 1950s.

Opposite: The guard house at Inverbervie, built from local stone, and with its design adapted to reflect the architectural style of the region.

Portland

It was intended that the Portland CEW station would be one of the first recipients of the advanced Type 80 radar, and the underground control bunker was modified during construction to incorporate a Kelvin-Hughes projector below the plotting room floor with a photographic display unit (PDU) in place of the manual plotting table. An American Type AN/FPS3 unit was installed, supposedly as an interim measure, until the Type 80 was available. The latter, in fact, was never installed and the Kelvin-Hughes well remained unoccupied. The station was closed in 1958.

Opposite above: The flat-roofed guard house at Portland was one of the few whose design was modified to incorporate local building materials.
Opposite below: At 65 feet the Portland bunker is the most deeply buried of all the Rotor control rooms. Because of this, access is via a lift rather than stairway. The view left is of the lower lift landing and on the right is a view from the lift looking down the access corridor into the bunker.
Right: Rotary converters and power supply switchgear in the underground powerhouse. Such plant are rare survivors in abandoned Rotor stations.
Below: Shortly before the bunker was sold in 2001 all the false floors were removed by the MoD for safety reasons. This is a view from the plotting room balcony looking down into the exposed Kelvin-Hughes chamber.

Above: The combined filter-plot room at Portland before the ill-conceived removal of the timber floor by the MoD in 2001. Before this act of official vandalism this was a unique example of a Phase One Rotor plotting room.

Trimingham

Trimingham opened as a CEW station in November 1952 and was refitted with a Type 80 radar in 1955. It continued as a CEW station under the 1958 plan (the successor to Rotor) and was also provided with a Type 54 Mk 3 radar enabling it to operate in the CHEL mode. The station was closed in 1961, but the site was re-acquired by the MoD in the late 1980s to provide a location for a remote Type 91 radar controlled from Neatishead. In 1997 the Type 90 was replaced by a Type 93 transferred from another former Rotor station at Hopton.

Right: The Type 93 radar protected by a Kevlar dome. Under the current scheme data from here is fed to Control and Reporting Centres at Boulmer and Scampton.

Below: Although the underground control centre is disused its guard house is still occupied by the RAF.

Overleaf: The abandoned plotting room in the underground R1 bunker at Trimingham showing the Kelvin-Hughes well.

TYPE R2 CHEL STATIONS

Chain Home Extra Low stations were established to track aircraft flying below the detection horizon of the Chain Home stations. They were provided with only one radar, either a Type 14 on a gantry or a Type 54 on a 200-foot mast.

Crosslaw

The station at Crosslaw, fitted with a Type 14 radar, came into service in October 1952. The CHEL stations were relatively simple (with only one radar head to contend with) and were provided with single level Type R2 underground bunkers.

Right: The guard house converted into a private residence.
Below left: The main spine corridor that gives access to all the principal rooms in the bunker.
Below right: The radar room abandoned and stripped of anything of value. Since closure the bunker has flooded to ceiling height in this room.

Goldsborough

Right: By 1957 it looked as though the advent of Type 80 radar would render the station redundant, but a disastrous fire in the underground operations room in March 1958 sealed its fate even before the official closure announcement was made. The guard house, which for many years was used as a hostel, was itself partially destroyed by fire in 2004. The underground bunker is flooded and inaccessible.

Hopton

Opening of the station at Hopton was delayed by six months due to a serious fire in the air-conditioning plant in 1953. The station was closed before 1960 and has subsequently suffered much vandalism, including a major fire in the bunker in 1984, after which the guard house was demolished and the bunker sealed.

In 1988 the land, which had been sold some fifteen years previously, was compulsorily purchased by the MoD and a Type 93 radar installed there, feeding data to Neatishead. This was removed in 1997 and the land once again sold. In 2000 the position of the stairwell to the underground bunker was located and subsequently excavated. It was found that all the plant and equipment had been removed from the bunker and it had suffered considerable fire damage.

Below: Investigations under way at the site of the stairwell leading to Hopton's underground operations centre.

Below: The plant room at Hopton, devoid of all evidence of the equipment once installed there.

TYPE R3 GCI STATIONS

Bawdsey

The R3 bunker at Bawdsey has a long and complex history. Scheduled for opening in January 1952, the site did not actually become operational until 1954. There were no less than ten radar heads on the site together with a Type 7 Mk3 on a remote R7 site just over a mile away on Alderton Marshes. An interim AN/FPS3 was supplemented in 1958 by a Type 80 radar.

In 1963 Bawdsey and Patrington were reclassified as Master Radar Stations but only a year later Bawdsey was reduced in status to a satellite to Neatishead. In 1966 the original classification was regained temporarily as a consequence of a disastrous fire in the R3 Control Centre at Neatishead. The latter station resumed control in 1974, after which Bawdsey was placed on care and maintenance.

Five years later in 1979 Bawdsey reopened as a Bloodhound Mk2 missile site with a new administration centre established in the former Rotor R3 bunker. The termination of the Bloodhound programme did not mark the end of Bawdsey. From 1984 to 1985 the underground bunker was refitted to serve as the Interim Alternative War Headquarters for RAF Strike Command while the new permanent Strike Command bunker was under construction at High Wycombe. In 1990 the bunker was finally abandoned and all the entrances filled with concrete. In recent years the bunker has twice been officially reopened for brief inspections.

Above right: Control equipment in the bunker's air-conditioning plant.

Bottom right: This 1960s manual telephone exchange still exists in good order in the bunker.

Below: The guard house modified with glazed panels to the veranda.

Above: An overhead view of the air-conditioning plant at Bawdsey, still in remarkably good condition after more than ten years of disuse.

Boulmer

Above: Very few of the many hundreds of nuclear bunkers built during the 1950s have survived intact until the present day, and fewer still continue to provide the functions for which they were first intended. One of these rare survivors is the Type R3 underground control bunker at the former GCI station at Boulmer in Northumberland.

Boulmer became fully operational, as one of twenty-five Rotor GCI stations, in September 1954. The early radar systems installed at many of the Rotor stations were quickly superseded by the technologically advanced Type 80 radar which, along with an associated projection display system, rendered redundant the original, double-level plotting room which had been the functional core of the original control room design. By 1958 the Rotor system was obsolete, but Boulmer survived as a Comprehensive GCI Station under the successor '1958 Plan', and subsequently took on the role of a Sector Operations Centre under the 1960s' Linesman/Mediator system. In 1974 the station was upgraded to become the Northern Sector Operations Centre, and a Control and Reporting Centre, under the United Kingdom Air Defence Ground Environment (UKADGE) scheme.

The original R3 bunker was substantially rebuilt in 1982. At that time, a new plant-room, decontamination suite and generators were added, and the earlier, double-level operations-well was floored over to provide two new, large operations rooms. The photograph above shows the Air Surveillance Suite in the Upper Operations Room, in 2005.

Buchan

The radar station at Buchan came into service in August 1953 and remains operational to the present day. Like many GCI stations it was initially provided with an interim AN/FPS3 radar until the Type 80 became available in 1956. A Type S259 was added in 1973 and remained operational until 1993. These radars were supplemented by an Argentinian TPS-43 unit captured during the Falklands war.

Buchan survived the demise of Rotor and became an integral part of the new United Kingdom Air Surveillance and Control System (UKASCS). In 1979 the existing R3 bunker was virtually doubled in size to provide space for the new standby generators and air-conditioning and filtration equipment required by the new high-powered radar.

Above: In 1988 a new Type 92 radar was installed at Buchan, protected by a Kevlar radome.

Left: The Rotor-period guard house at Buchan, another example of the standard design adapted to reflect the local architectural style and built with local materials.

Holmpton (Patrington)

Above: The installation of Type 80 radar at GCI stations required some modification of the control bunker to accommodate the Kelvin-Hughes projector and associated Photographic Display Unit. The PDU shown here is located in the new operations room situated at the far end of the bunker from the original double-level plotting room. Holmpton was classified as a Master Radar Station under the 1958 plan. The bunker at Holmpton is now a popular tourist attraction and has the only surviving intact Kelvin-Hughes PDU.

Neatishead

Above: A Type 84 radar at Neatishead, the last surviving fixed Cold War radar, installed between 1962 and 1964. At much the same time work began on a massive R12 bunker on the surface on top of which was mounted the 60-feet-wide dish of a Type 85 high power surveillance radar. Shortly afterwards, major alterations were made to the earlier R3 operations room at Neatishead, including the addition of a third floor to accommodate the necessary power and ventilation plants.

Opposite: Standard Local Early Warning and Control (SLEWC) consoles and glazed tote board preserved in the operations room at Neatishead. This was set up in the former Second World War Happidrome following a fire in the R3 bunker in 1966, in which three civilian fire-fighters lost their lives. The Happidrome was redesignated as an R30, and remained in use until the R3 was refurbished. The R30 is now part of the Air Defence Radar Museum.

Above and below: Two views of the air-conditioning plant at Neatishead.

Above right: Three standby generators in the Neatishead powerhouse.

Below right: Banks of air filters – part of the station's ventillation system.

Skendleby

Above: The GCI station at Skendleby came into service in July 1953. Between 1964 and 1968 the bunker served as the Lincolnshire County Civil Defence Control. In 1968 it became a Home Office Sub-Regional Control.

In 1985 the bunker underwent a radical reconstruction and acquired a new lease of life as a Regional Government Headquarters for the East Midlands Region, with the designation RGHQ 3.1. The reconstruction involved the insertion of a third floor in the body of the R3 bunker (made possible by the existence of very deep service ducts between the two original floors), and the building of a fourth floor on top of the original structure. The latter was, in fact, constructed at ground level and subsequently covered with a deep earth mound.

The new upper floor consists of a plant-room containing the standby diesel generators together with ventilation fans which draw in external air through banks of charcoal filters, and exhaust stale air via the ventilation towers visible in the photograph above.

Above and below: Kitchen and catering facilities at Skendleby, provided to the usual high standard found in all the 1980s Regional Government Headquarters.

Above: A typical example of the office space available in the RGHQ.

Below: The new plant-room emergency exit with ventilation towers above.

Sopley

The GCI station at Sopley became operational in the summer of 1954. A Type 80 radar was installed in 1956. As well as being more discriminating and resilient to jamming, the Type 80 extended the detecting range of the station from about 90 miles to in excess of 320 miles.

No longer required for Rotor after 1958, the station continued in existence in a number of roles connected with joint civilian and military air traffic control services. This came to and end in 1974 with the introduction of the Linesman/ Mediator air traffic control (ATC) system with its new control centre at West Drayton.

In the early 1980s work began on the conversion of the bunker to serve as a temporary emergency operations room for the Headquarters of UK Land Forces while a permanent operations room was under construction at UKLFHQ at Wilton near Salisbury. The Sopley bunker was sold into the private sector in 1993.

Above: The guard house at Sopley, unusual in that it does not have a pitched roof.

Right: A view up the emergency exit staircase from the bunker.

Wartling

Wartling entered service late, in March 1955, and survived beyond the Rotor era to function as one of six Master Radar Stations under the 1958 scheme. The station's role was taken over by RAF Bawdsey, and by 1976 the whole site had passed into private hands. The guard house was subsequently converted into a private residence.

Above: The remains of the Photographic Display Unit associated with the Kelvin-Hughes projector installed at Wartling when the station was equipped with Type 80 radar in 1957. Although badly vandalised this is of historical importance because it is the only example of its type surviving in situ.

In the pit below, high-speed cameras recorded images from high intensity radar displays at the rate of one every 15 seconds (one revolution of the antenna). Each frame was processed and projected onto the PDU with a delay of just one minute.

Above: After closure the bunker became susceptible to flooding, and by 1997 the water had reached a depth of almost eight feet. In 2004 a major operation was put in place by members of *Subterranea Britannica* to pump water out of the bunker in order to make a photographic record. This photograph shows the original two-level operations room partially cleared of flood water. When visited in 2010 the water level had risen to the top of the steps.

Above: An under-side view of the Photographic Display Unit.

Below: Switchgear in the flooded plant-room in 1987. By 2004 the water level had reached the top of the ladder.

Above: Intercept Cabin No.1, overlooking the operations room with the situation board still in place.

Below: A concrete mounting plinth for one of the air-conditioning compressors, removed from the plant-room after closure.

Above right and left: A circulating fan and air filtration unit in the bunker's ventilation plant.

Below: Wartling's Type 80 modulator building, now converted into a private dwelling.

TYPE R6 GCI STATIONS

Hope Cove

The GCI station at Hope Cove on the Devon coast was operational for less than two years. In September 1957, it became briefly the RAF Fighter Control School. In October 1958 it was transferred to the Home Office for conversion into a Regional Seat of Government (RSG7) controlling the southwest of England. The nearby Second World War 'Happidrome' was adapted at the same time to provide additional accommodation. In 1989 the 'Happidrome' was demolished and at much the same time the function of the bunker, by now reclassified as RGHQ 7.2, was transferred to a new regional headquarters bunker recently completed at Chilmark near Salisbury. The site was sold to a private owner in 2000.

Above: An external view of the upper floor of the semi-submerged R6 bunker at Hope Cove. Notice the prominent ventilation outlet duct on the corner of the building.

Right: A view of the upper-floor spine corridor within the bunker. Through continued usage in various guises the building has survived in remarkably good condition. Notice the station identification plaque on the left-hand wall.

Above: When photographed in April 2000 the original 1950s air-conditioning plant seen here was still in perfect working order.

Above: The Type 80 modulator building at Hope Cove, now used as an agricultural fodder store.

Below: The station's standby generator. This is contained within a separate building linked to the main bunker by an enclosed walkway.

Below: A small kitchen dating from the time of the bunker's role as a Regional Government Headquarters.

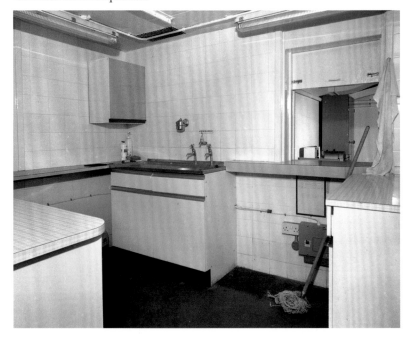

Langtoft

The GCI station at Langtoft in Lincolnshire was unusual in that although it was located on the vulnerable east coast, it was provided with a semi-submerged R6 bunker rather than the more usual completely underground R3 type.

The station came into service in July 1953 with a compliment of nine radar heads including an R7. A Type 80 modulator building was erected around 1956 but there is little evidence that it was fitted out or the new radar ever installed. The station was closed down and put under care and maintenance in March 1958.

Above: The R6 bunker still survives and is used as a store in the middle of an extensive scrap yard. A wartime 'Happidrome' also survives nearby together with a number of Rotor-period radar plinths.

Right: The two-level operations room of the R6 bunker now filled with scrap metal.

St Twynnells

The GCI station at St Twynnells on the Pembroke Peninsula was the last to be completed and its future looked doubtful even while building was in progress. By that time it was evident that the far superior Type 80 radar would supersede the Type 7 and Type 14 radars that had been earmarked for installation at this site.

A Type 80 was scheduled for inclusion at St Twynnells and a modulator building was erected, but the station was deleted from the Rotor scheme before this plan was put into effect. Ultimately, the only search radar installed at St Twynnells was a mobile Type 11 Mk7 and it is unlikely that the station was ever fully operational.

Above: The R6 bunker with the separate standby set house to the left and a transformer building to the right.

Right: The tote board in the two-level operations room.

Above: In the background is the Type 80 modulator building with a Type 13 radar plinth in the foreground.

Below left: Intercept Cabin No.1, with the false floor removed.
Below right: The radar office. Removal of the false floor has revealed the extensive air ducts needed to cool the valve-powered radar electronics.

Treleaver

Above: The remains of the R6 bunker at Treleaver in west Cornwall.
Below: The partially flooded floor of the control room.
Right: A derelict circulating fan in the air-conditioning plant-room.

TYPE R8 GCI STATIONS

Charmy Down

Below: Charmy Down was one of a series of 'readiness' GCI stations that were not given the high priority in the Rotor funding schedule. Most of these sites were located in the less vulnerable parts of the country and, as an economy measure – for Rotor was proving extortionately expensive – they were provided with only light-weight prefabricated control buildings which provided no blast or fall-out protection at all.

Building began in May 1953 but the station was still incomplete when construction was halted in April 1955 after some £200,000 had been spent

on it. Aerial photographs indicate that at least the shells of the buildings had been completed, and the existence of cable trenches between the radar heads suggests that preliminary fitting-out had been started. There is no evidence, however, that the seven radar heads earmarked for the site were ever installed or that any electronic equipment was installed in the operations block.

All that survives at the Charmy Down site, situated on a Second World War airfield just to the east of Bath, are a number of brick radar plinths, a transformer building and the concrete foundation of the R8 operations block. Associated with these foundations is a concrete ramp on brick piers which allowed heavy radar equipment to be hauled up into the elevated radar office.

Chenies

Above: The surviving R8 operations block at Chenies in Hertfordshire. Note the inclined equipment ramp similar to that at Charmy Down.

Below left and right: The standby set house and diesel generator at Chenies. The Kevlar dome in the background protects a Meteorological Office radar located at the same site.

Right: The well-preserved tote board in the operations room at Chenies. This has now been dismantled and installed in the R3 museum at Holmpton. The GCI station closed in 1957 but continued for many years in MoD hands, functioning as a Strike Command communications facility. The operations block was used until the late 1990s as a sports hall.

Killard Point

The GCI station at Killard Point in County Down, Northern Ireland, was established as part of the last stage of the Rotor programme, designed to extend radar coverage around the northwest of Scotland and the Western Approaches. It was intended that the station should be fitted with a Type 84 radar under the 1958 plan, but this was not followed up.

Below: Surviving Rotor radar plinths at Killard Point.

Wick

Right: The remains of the R8 operations block at Wick in Caithness, Scotland. The station at Wick was one of two GCI stations built under the Rotor 3 plan, to extend radar coverage over the north and west of the British Isles. The other Rotor 3 GCI station was at Killard Point in Northern Ireland. It would appear that the site at Wick was never fitted-out or brought into service.

Much of the R8 block has been demolished but the section seen here survives as a car repair workshop. The Type 80 modulator building and standby set house remain largely intact.

TYPE R10 ROTOR 3 CEW STATIONS

Faraid Head

Below: Faraid Head was one of the last Rotor stations to be built, with a target completion date of 1956. By the end of the following year it had been deleted from the Rotor programme. A Type 80 modulator building was constructed (and still survives as the control building for the Cape Wrath Naval Range), but it is unlikely that the radar was ever installed. Little else remains at Faraid Head other than a few concrete foundations.

Saxa Vord

The Rotor stage 3 CEW station at Saxa Vord came on stream towards the end of 1956. Completion was delayed because the Type 80 radar array was blown off its mounting in a 120 mph storm that winter.

Below left: The later, R101, radar beneath its radome at Saxa Vord.

Above and below right: The station was provided with a brick-built R10 control bunker which still survives although now disused. Saxa Vord continues to function as a Reporting Post for the United Kingdom Air Surveillance and Control System (UKASCS). The site now has no radar but is retained as a communications and download link.

TYPE R11 ROTOR 3 CHEL STATIONS

Five new CHEL stations were proposed under the final Rotor 3 programme, located at Kilchiaran, Murlough Bay, West Myne, Snaefell and Prestatyn. Each would be provided with a brick-built R11 control bunker similar in layout to the underground CHEL R2 type.

None saw much, if any, active life as construction was not begun until 1956 and all were closed down by 1958.

Snaefell

Right: The R11 bunker near the summit of Snaefell on the Isle of Man was used as a motor cycle museum for many years but this has now closed.

Prestatyn

Above: The spectacularly located R11 bunker at Prestatyn. Long disused, the building has been bricked up and remains in remarkably good condition. The building behind the main bunker, adjacent to the BT microwave tower, is the station's standby generator building.

Chapter 5

RADAR CONTROL & REPORTING CENTRES

Portreath

Above: The Control and Reporting Post bunker at RAF Portreath on the north Cornwall coast, on the site of the former Nancekuke chemical weapons factory.

Under the 1971 UKADGE scheme the site at Portreath was selected as one of a series of control and reporting posts. When opened in 1980 it was provided with a Type 93 radar, now upgraded to a Type 101. The control bunker was built in 1988 and extended in 1992.

Above: The air-conditioning plant at Portreath.

Following the advent of the Type 90 series mobile radars, the number of existing stations was reduced and re-organised into two sectors. The northern sector SOC/CRC was at Buchan (R3), with a CRC at Boulmer (R3) and CRPs at Benbecula and Saxa Vord. The southern SOC/CRC was at Neatishead (R3), with CRPs at Portreath and Staxton Wold. There was also a mobile radar at Ty Croes on Anglesey. A further southern sector CRP, at Bishopscourt in Northern Ireland, was closed in the 1990s. This organisation has since been further refined into what is the current UKASACS system, with of an underground CRC (R3) at Boulmer, and a surface CRC at Scampton supported by Remote Radar Heads (RRHs) at Portreath, Trimingham (Neatishead's remote radar), Staxton Wold, Buchan and Benbecula.

Portreath

Above: The Type 101 radar, enclosed in its protective dome, at RAF Portreath.

Staxton Wold

Below: The 1980s Control and Reporting Post building at Staxton Wold.

Above: During the early 1960s Type 84 and Type 85 radars were installed at Staxton Wold as well as two HF200 height-finding radars.

The Type 85 radar was mounted on top of a massive, three-storey R12 bunker. The lower storey consisted of a sub-ground basement. The electronic equipment in the bunker generated huge amounts of heat which required an extensive cooling and ventilating system. Much of this equipment was housed in a single-storey extension attached to one side of the main building.

The photograph above shows control consoles within the R12 building at Staxton Wold. Some of the equipment, including the radar monitors, has been removed. The R12 bunker was demolished in the summer of 2010.

Above: The 1960s R12 control bunker at Staxton Wold. The Type 85 radar was mounted on the roof of the projecting central bay on the right.

Below: Type 93 mobile radar beneath its radome at Staxton Wold.

Chapter 6

ANTI-AIRCRAFT OPERATIONS ROOMS

In the early 1950s anti-aircraft guns were still considered a credible defence against piston-engined bombers. Following an increase in tension with the Soviet Union at the outbreak of the Korean War, Britain's anti-aircraft defences were rehabilitated. At thirty-two key 'Gun Defended Areas' (GDAs) new gun sites were established or existing Second World War sites upgraded. Most GDAs were provided with a two-storey Anti-Aircraft Operations Room. The majority became operational in 1952 but within three years the advent of high-altitude jet bombers and ballistic missiles rendered them obsolete and all were abandoned in March 1955.

Torrance House

Below: The AAOR at Torrance House in East Kilbride controlled the Clyde GDA. After a few years of disuse the AAOR found a role from the mid-1960s in the Scottish Emergency Government structure, serving intermittently as the Scottish Western Zone Headquarters until 1983. It is now used as a country park storage facility.

Campsie

Left: Set in a disused quarry, the AAOR at Campsie was intended to control the guns of the Londonderry GDA.

Although the concrete shell of the AAOR was completed it was never fitted out. Originally this bunker was to have controlled the Londonderry guns and another, at Lisburn, would have controlled guns in the Belfast GDA. A change of priorities within Anti-Aircraft Command resulted in the Lisburn AAOR taking control of both GDAs, and the abandonment of the Campsie bunker.

Below left: A view of the interior of the bunker which illustrates the early stage at which the building work was prematurely ended.

Below right: The unfinished two-storey operations room. Girders were erected for the gallery but this was never completed. The building is now used as an animal shelter.

Craigiehall

Below left and right: Two views of the operations room at Craigiehall, adapted for use as a conference and lecture hall.

Above: The AAOR at Craigiehall controlled the Forth and Rosyth GDA. It stands within the grounds of the Headquarters 2nd Division British Army in Scotland and is used as a conference and training facility.

Fareham

Above: An ad hoc operations room was established in the north barrack block of Fort Fareham, one of the series of so-called Palmerston Forts built in the 1860s to resist an anticipated French invasion. This was intended as an interim measure until a permanent AAOR was constructed. Building work on the proposed new bunker, however, had not begun before Anti-Aircraft Command was wound-up.

Frodsham

Right: Most AAORs were built to one of two standard designs: either built completely on the surface or with one floor underground. In the latter design both entrances are on the upper floor. At just two locations, here at Frodsham and at Worsley near Manchester, the bunker is built into a hillside and has one entrance on each floor.

Built to control the Mersey GDA, the bunker was transferred to Cheshire County Council in 1962 and functioned as the Northwich Civil Defence Sub-Control until 1968. Frodsham remained in service as the Cheshire standby control until 1991 and is still retained for civil emergencies.

Below left: The operations room at Frodsham.

Below right: Raynet equipment in the Emergency Centre's radio room.

Elvaston

Above: The semi-underground AAOR bunker at Elvaston, which commanded the Derby GDA.

Gosforth

Left: The Gosforth AAOR in the northern suburbs of Newcastle upon Tyne once controlled the guns of the Tyne GDA. From 1965 to 1968 it was the Northumberland County Southeast Area Control and, since the mid-1970s, has been the home of the Northumberland County Archives.

Inverkip

Above and opposite: Situated close to the Langhouse Hotel, the Inverkip AAOR controlled the gun-sites protecting the Clyde Anchorage. Taken over by the Admiralty shortly after the winding-down of Anti-Aircraft Command, the bunker served up until the mid-1970s as a Navy Control Centre known as HMS *Dalriada*. At some time in the 1980s the bunker suffered a serious fire, confined mainly to the wooden balcony. Efforts by the local fire brigade to contain the fire resulted in the lower floor flooding to a depth of fifteen inches. Seepage water has caused the flooding to increase over the years. In April 2010 a planning application was submitted for conversion of the bunker into a single dwelling.

Below: The remains of the bunker's original plotting table in a room on the flooded lower floor. Notice the 'Aircraft State' board on the wall.

Below: A view from the flooded control room looking up towards the fire-damaged balcony.

Kirklevington Hall

Above: The AAOR for the Teeside GDA stands in the grounds of the Kirklevington Hotel and has in recent years been converted into a private house.

Llanion Barracks

Below left and right: The Milford Haven GDA was controlled from a non-standard AAOR constructed in the former powder magazine of the Victorian Llanion barracks. The wooden balcony has collapsed during the last decade.

Lisburn

Above: The AAOR for the Belfast GDA at Lisburn was adapted in 1963 as the Belfast (No.31 Group) ROC Headquarters. At that time the front entrance was extended and a new air-conditioning plant installed. More recently, the bunker was home to the British Army's main communications centre for Northern Ireland.

Landguard

Below left and right: An interim AAOR was established in the left battery at Landguard Fort to control the Harwich GDA while the permanent bunker at Mistley was under construction.

Lansdown

Above: The AAOR for the Bristol GDA, located at Lansdown near Bath, was handed over to the Royal Observer Corps in 1959 to become the Headquarters for No.12 Group. Some years later the Southern Sector UKWMO transferred from RAF Rudloe Manor to be co-located with the ROC at Lansdown. In 1992 the bunker and adjacent modern administration block were taken over by Avon Fire Brigade.

Left: The balcony, seen here during Avon Fire Brigade's tenure, was altered when the building was occupied by the ROC. The curved glass panels were removed at that time.

Ridgeway Hill   *Above:* The operations room of the Portland GDA at Ridgeway Hill overlooking Weymouth has in recent years been used as a toy-dealer's warehouse. Following the winding-up of Anti-Aircraft Command in 1955 the bunker was handed over to the Royal Navy and was used as an Admiralty chart store until shortly before its sale in 1998.

Above: Exterior view of the Ridgeway Hill AAOR.

Ullenwood

Left: The semi-underground bunker at Ullenwood near Cheltenham controlled the guns of the Brockworth GDA.

In 1965 it became the Group Headquarters for Gloucester Civil Defence and later, in 1968, became one of two Sub-Regional Controls (along with Hope Cove in Devon) for the South West Region. Subsequently it became the region's SRHQ until usurped around 1985 by a new bunker at Chilmark.

Above and below: The Ullenwood AAOR has survived in remarkably good condition and is one of only a few that have retained their original curved glass balcony glazing.

In 1992 the bunker was acquired by Gloucestershire County Archives for use as a store, and in 2000 was transferred to Gloucester Trading Standards. It was used as a training centre by Gloucester Fire Brigade until about 2005 when the site was sold for redevelopment. A house is built on the land but the bunker is largely unaltered and is now used for storage.

Uxbridge

Above: In 1962 the AAOR at Uxbridge was transferred to the United States Airforce to become one of the two joint hubs of the US Autovon military communications network. A new external powerhouse was built at that time to house a pair of standby generators.

Below: Telecomms equipment room inside the main bunker.

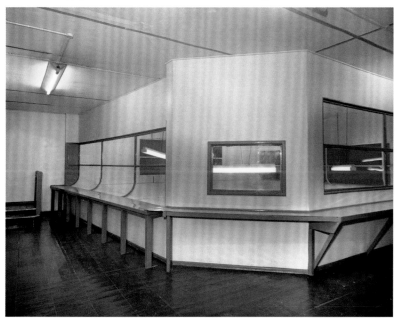

Uxbridge

Above: The Uxbridge AAOR was probably the last to be built on the UK mainland. A change in priority for the West London GDA resulted in a delay in construction and it is probable that fitting-out had still not begun when Anti-Aircraft Command was wound up in 1955. In 1959 it was proposed that the bunker should become a launch co-ordination centre for the Blue Streak missile system, but the project was cancelled before any work was done.

Following its acquisition by the US Airforce in 1962 considerable alterations and additions were made, but the original outline of the building is still discernible.

Vange

Above: The AAOR for the North Thames GDA is situated at Marsh Farm near Basildon in Essex.

Below left and right: The bunker has been used in recent years as a paint-ball venue and has suffered considerable damage, including the loss of the balcony glazing. The lower floor is subject to water ingress and is partially flooded. The bunker is now an airsoft venue known as Bunker CQB.

Wenallt

The Wenallt AAOR which formerly controlled the guns of the Cardiff GDA was acquired in the 1970s by British Telecom for conversion into the BT War Headquarters for Wales. Although some equipment was moved into the bunker and new facilities including kitchens and dormitories provided, the work was never completed. In recent years the bunker has been badly vandalised.

Left: The operations room at Wenallt, showing the uncompleted conversion work undertaken by British Telecom.

Below left: A two-position manual switchboard, delivered to Wenallt but never installed.

Below right: The standby generator and associated switchgear.

West Cross   *Above:* The Swansea GDA operations room at West Cross is currently the home of the Joint Emergency Planning Unit for Bridgend, Neath, Port Talbot and the City and County of Swansea.

West Cross

Above: The rather bleak exterior of the Swansea AAOR at West Cross.

Wawne

Below right: The AAOR at Wawne formerly controlled the guns of the Hull GDA and was later used as an Emergency Planning Centre by the now defunct Humberside County Council.

Below left: In recent years the bunker has served as a police training and conference centre, but has now been converted into two dwellings.

Worsley

Above: Situated on the site of Worsley New Hall, a country house demolished shortly after the First World War, the AAOR at Worsley controlled the guns of the Manchester GDA.

Like the similar structure at Frodsham in Cheshire, the Worsley bunker is built into a slight hillside and has one entrance on each level.

Following the end of Anti-Aircraft Command the bunker was transferred to the Admiralty and served as a Navy food store administered by RNSD Risley.

In 1961 the bunker was acquired by Salford Corporation who used it as a Joint Area Control with Lancashire County Council. In 1966 it became a Civil Defence Sub-Area Control for Stretford and Turton. After several years under care and maintenance following the demise of Civil Defence in 1968 the bunker was transferred to Greater Manchester Fire Service in 1974.

The site was eventually sold into the private sector in the early 1990s and was occupied for many years by a gun club.

Worsley

Above: A side view of the Worsley bunker, now almost engulfed by surrounding woodland.

Below left and right: Shortly after the gun club left in around 2002, the bunker was broken into and has subsequently never been made properly secure. As a consequence the interior has been badly vandalised.

Chapter 7

ROYAL OBSERVER CORPS GROUP HEADQUARTERS

Goosnargh

Above: The semi-underground structure at Goosnargh was one of a group of three similar bunkers on the same site, built in the early 1940s to provide an operations room and a communications centre for No.9 Group RAF Fighter Command. The bunker became the ROC Western Area Group Control Centre in January 1962 and, in 1973, became home also to the Western

Sector Control Centre of the United Kingdom Warning and Monitoring Organisation. UKWMO was formed by the integration of the Air Raid Warning Organisation and the ROC, and its role was to warn of air attack, to confirm nuclear strikes, and to set off public warning of both air attack and of approaching fallout. Confirmation by UKWMO of a nuclear attack would also have been instrumental in the immediate scrambling of the RAF V-Bomber force in preparation for nuclear retaliation.

Around 1985 the Goosnargh bunker became the standby UKWMO Headquarters as well as a Sector Headquarters. At that time the bunker was refitted and the new plant-room extension was added. UKWMO was disbanded in 1991 and shortly afterwards the bunker found a new function, albeit only briefly, as an RGHQ for Region 10.

Bunker provision in Region 10 had been far from adequate. The RSG was located at Preston barracks and, from the late 1960s, there was a single-storey Sub-Regional Control beneath a new government office block in Southport. This later became SRHQ 10.1 but was abandoned in the early 1980s due to recurrent flooding. RGHQ 10.2 was established in a former Rotor GCI bunker at Hack Green in Cheshire, which was extensively refurbished for the purpose. From its inception the Hack Green bunker, in theory, accommodated both of the Region 10 RGHQs, although in practice, due to its limited staff accommodation, its only joint function was as a communications link to the county emergency centres within its region. The problem of limited accommodation was solved in 1991 when the recently vacated ROC bunker at Goosnargh was redesignated as RGHQ 10.1. Conversion work was completed in 1992, but within a year, as a consequence of the end of the Cold War, the whole RGHQ concept was abandoned.

Above: One of the two generators in the new (circa 1985) plant room, its control gear already partially dismantled following the bunker's closure in 1992.

Below: The control room of No.21 Group ROC, Preston, in the Goosnargh bunker, viewed from the balcony. By the time this photograph was taken the original control room was out of use, hence the new offices built in the well. From 1973, the ROC control was co-located with UKWMO Sector Control in a new control room elsewhere in the bunker.

Below: Air-conditioning control equipment in the new plant-room.

Acomb

Above: The semi-underground 'Aztec temple' pattern control bunker for No.20 Group ROC, York, at Acomb near York. This is one of two standard designs of ROC Group Controls. The bunker has been fully restored by English Heritage and is open to the public.

Knavesmire

Below: The Second World War ROC Group Control at Knavesmire, in the outskirts of York, was briefly brought back into service to serve No.20 Group until the new bunker at Acomb was completed in 1961. It is currently occupied by a rugby club.

Acomb

Above: A view from the balcony looking down on to the control table in the operations room at Acomb before restoration. The original perspex 'B' display is still in position but the 'A' display has been transferred to the Imperial War Museum.

Note also the right-hand vertical 'T' display upon which is mounted a nationwide map of monitoring posts. On the balcony above the 'T' display can be seen the swivelling tote boards by means of which current information could be relayed to the operators below.

Oban

Above: The above-ground alternative design of bunker provided for No.27 Group ROC at Oban. Opened in May 1962, the bunker closed in 1973 when its posts were transferred to No.30 Group. The bunker acted as a sub-AFHQ for Highland Regional Council from the mid-1980s until 1991. The bunker was sold by Defence Estates in August 2009.

Ayr

Below: The No.25 Group ROC, Ayr, control at Waterloo Road in Prestwick was built to the same design as that at Oban but, like a few others, was later clad in heavy-gauge corrugated steel sheeting. The building was demolished in 2001 to make way for a car park.

Carmarthen

Above: The corrugated-steel-clad bunker for No.13 Group ROC opened in December 1961 and closed in 1992. From 1992 to 2000 it was leased to the Carmarthen Civil Protection Unit. The views *(below left and right)* show the control room in 2001 shortly after the end of the Protection Unit's tenure. The bunker has now been demolished.

Fiskerton

Above: The 'Aztec temple' pattern semi-underground bunker provided at Fiskerton for No.15 Group ROC, Lincoln, came into service in 1960. Disused for several years following its closure in 1992, it was purchased in 1998 by a company involved in the manufacture of specialist ammunition, principally supplied to a number of police forces. The bunker is apparently equipped as a rapid intervention skills police training facility.

Maidstone

Opposite: The three-level 'Aztec temple' control for No.1 Group ROC, Maidstone, stands in the grounds of Ashmore House and was opened in June 1960. Following its closure in 1992 many of its contents were sold to the Cold War museum at Kelvedon Hatch in Essex. The bunker, which remains in excellent condition, was until recently used as a document store by the firm of solicitors that now owns it. It is now empty and occasional public tours are run by Maidstone museum.

Right: Air-conditioning compressors in the plant room at Maidstone.

Horsham

Below: Located in Denne Road, Horsham, the control centre for No.2 Group ROC, Horsham, was built to the standard brick-clad surface design, but with a large extension on the left side, added in 1973, to accommodate the UKWMO Metropolitan Sector Control which was co-located there. Opened in April 1962 and closed in 1992, the bunker was demolished in 2004.

Norwich

Above: The control for No.6 Group ROC, Norwich, in Chartwell Road, Old Catton, was opened in September 1961, closed in 1992 and demolished in 2008.

Truro

Left: The control centre for No.11 Group ROC, located in Daniel Street in Truro, was opened in May 1963 and closed in March 1973 at which time its monitoring posts were transferred to No.10 Group.

The bunker was placed under care and maintenance until June 1975 when it was reopened as a Nuclear Reporting Cell for St Mawgan and Culdrose. The Nuclear Reporting Cell remained in use until 1995, after which the bunker was closed down.

The two-storey surface building was built to the standard design, part-rendered and part-faced in local granite.

Between 1995 and 2001 the adjacent administration block was used as a driving test centre. The entire site was demolished in 2003.

Poltimore

Above: Located at Poltimore Park close to the M4 motorway, the No.10 Group ROC, Exeter, control bunker shares a compound with a Second World War RAF Fighter Command Sector Operations Room.

Below left: Still in good condition when it was sold in 1996, the bunker was subsequently broken into and the control room badly vandalised.

Below right: The air-conditioning and generator plant rooms showed very little sign of deterioration when this photograph was taken in November 1999.

School Hill

In 1964 the protected transmitter block of a former Second World War Chain Home radar station was converted to provide accommodation for the UKWMO Caledonian Sector Control which had previously been located at the Barnton Quarry SOC. UKWMO remained at School Hill until 1976 when it was relocated to the No.28 Group ROC, Dundee, control at Craigiebarns.

Grampian Fire Brigade has occupied the bunker since 1978, using it as a training centre for off-shore fire-fighting on North Sea oil rigs.

Left: The control room at School Hill looking the worse for wear in the summer of 2004.

Opposite: The control room at Poltimore, looking towards the balcony, in 1999. The local planning authority intimated when the bunker was sold by the government that they would only agree either to its use as a museum or else its demolition. In 2006 they relented and the bunker is now used as a paintball venue.

Watford

A new semi-underground control bunker was built for No.5 Group ROC, Watford, at Cassiobury Drive, Watford in 1961 adjacent to the Second World War ROC Headquarters. No.5 Group was disbanded in 1968 but the bunker was retained as a secondary training centre until 1973.

Left: The Second World War Headquarters, now used as a surgery by the Park Veterinary Centre.

Below left: Pneumatic sewage-ejectors in the post-war bunker.

Below right: The bunker's spine corridor looking towards the emergency exit.

Above: The 1961 control bunker at Watford survives in remarkably good condition and is currently used for storage by the nearby veterinary practice.

Yeovil

A new control bunker for No.9 Group ROC, Yeovil, was opened on the site of an existing Second World War ROC centre at Hendford Hill in November 1963.

After stand down in 1991 the bunker was retained by the Home Office for use as a nodal point in the Emergency Communications Network.

Generally referred to as the 'G-CAT Computer Centre', probably to confuse inquisitive local residents, the bunker was fitted out with a range of new communications equipment including an SX2000 switching unit and a suite of computer terminals, along with a new standby generator.

The Home Office proposed the closure and sale of the bunker in the mid-1990s but a suitable buyer could not be found. The bunker remained in Home Office hands until 2001, the ECN equipment having undergone a major upgrade just two years previously.

Above: The bunker at Hendford Hill is built into a sloping hillside. On the lower ground to the west the surviving Second World War huts were retained for use as an administration centre.

Left: The new standby generator positioned in the bunker's former decontamination unit.

Chapter 8

ROYAL OBSERVER CORPS MONITORING POSTS

Following the reinstatement of the ROC in 1951, plans were made for the provision of new observation posts built to a standard design that offered better protection than the assorted jumble of existing posts. A total of 413 such posts, manufactured by the Orlit company of Colnbrook, were erected over the next three years. By 1955, however, the danger from radioactive fallout was better understood and it was realised that better-protected accommodation was required and, in May 1956, the construction of the first of an eventual 1,563 underground monitoring posts was begun. Each three-man post was equipped with simple instruments that could record the power and direction of nuclear detonations and determine the level of radiation in dust clouds. Reports relayed by a number of posts to their Group Controls would generate an accurate overview of the regional situation.

Lutterworth

Below: The ventilation shafts, mounting points for external instruments and, in the background, the open hatch of the access shaft, are all that is visible of the underground post at Lutterworth in Leicestershire. The post was demolished and the site redeveloped in 2000.

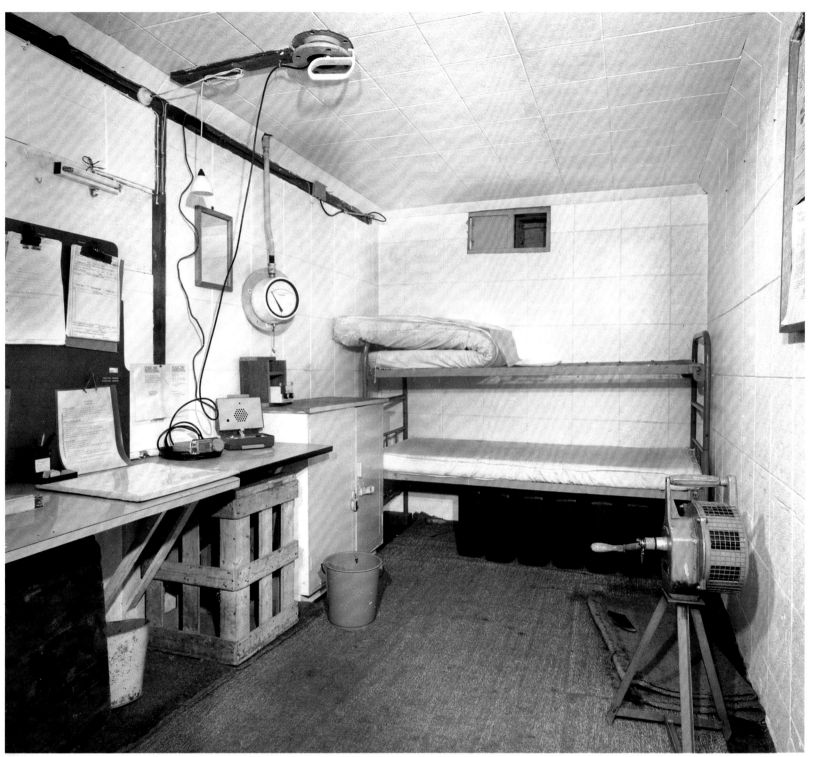

Knockholt

Above: The compact interior of the underground post at Knockholt in Kent. Note the dial of the bomb-power indicator (BPI) mounted on the left-hand wall, and the orange PDRM 82(F) fixed survey meter on the desk below. The adjacent yellow and blue instrument is an AD8010 Teletalk, which enabled direct voice communication with the post's Group Control.

Two types of 'Orlit' posts were built: type 'A', which was usually constructed on the ground, and type 'B' which was supported on six-foot concrete legs.

Chard

Right: The type 'B' Orlit post at Chard with its replacement underground post in the foreground. One of every cluster of underground posts was designated a Master Post and provided with radio communication. The aerial connection on the side of the ventilator shaft at Chard indicates that this was a Master Post.

Bigbury-on-Sea

Below: This view of the rather weather-beaten type 'B' Orlit post at Bigbury-on-Sea shows the short, metal-runged ladder giving access to the entrance. The site was unsuitable for an underground post, which was built at Holberton.

Tunstall

Below: Unusually, the type 'A' Orlit post at Tunstall in Yorkshire was built on top of a Second World War pillbox. The Ground Zero Indicator (GZI) mounting pillar for the nearby underground post that replaced it has been incorporated into the corner of the Orlit post.

Redditch
Above: The post at Redditch was built on the edge of a sandpit. After closure, sand extraction resumed resulting in the land around the post falling away to reveal its external structure.

Modbury
Below: Probably due to poor surrounding visibility, the post at Modbury in Devon was provided with an unusually high GZI pillar accessed by a short flight of four concrete steps.

Cley-next-the-Sea
Below: At Cley-next-the-Sea in Norfolk the sloping ground has been cut away on one side of the bunker and a door and window inserted to provide a bird hide for the Norfolk Ornithology Association who acquired the site in 1975.

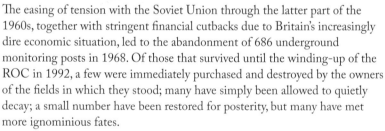

The easing of tension with the Soviet Union through the latter part of the 1960s, together with stringent financial cutbacks due to Britain's increasingly dire economic situation, led to the abandonment of 686 underground monitoring posts in 1968. Of those that survived until the winding-up of the ROC in 1992, a few were immediately purchased and destroyed by the owners of the fields in which they stood; many have simply been allowed to quietly decay; a small number have been restored for posterity, but many have met more ignominious fates.

Draperstown

Above: The underground post at Draperstown in Londonderry is widely believed to have been destroyed in an arson attack by the IRA in 1987. Due to its vulnerable location it was abandoned and never rebuilt or replaced.

Plympton

Above right: The post at Plympton in Devon was one of those made redundant by the first round of closures in 1968 and was declared surplus in October of that year. It remained intact, however, with many of its fittings still in place until the late 1990s when it was destroyed by fire.

Spondon

Right: At Spondon in Derbyshire the underground post, another of the casualties of 1968, was used during the 1980s by a group of local amateur-radio enthusiasts as an unofficial VHF repeater station. The bunker is now flooded to a depth of two feet.

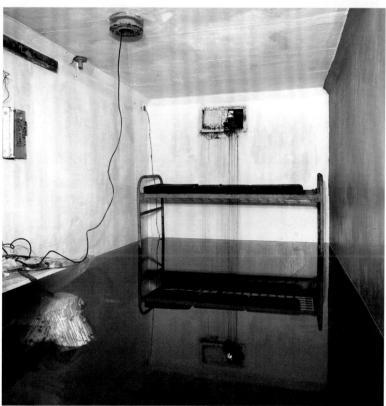

Chapter 9

CHANNEL ISLANDS CIVIL PROTECTION

Although Civil Defence was stood down on the British mainland in 1968, it is still active, under the title of 'Civil Protection', in the Channel Islands, with control centres in Guernsey, Jersey and Alderney, all located in German bunkers dating from the Second World War.

Alderney

Right: The Alderney Civil Protection control is housed in a former German ammunition bunker, later adapted by the German Army to function as its central surgical unit. The two-storey bunker on Longis Road is shared with the Royal Alderney Militia, an organization of ancient origin, reconstituted in the 1980s by a retired SAS officer. The Civil Protection function operates under the jurisdiction of Guernsey and a monitoring post in the bunker reports to the Guernsey headquarters.

Guernsey

Below left: The two-storey Guernsey Civil Protection headquarters, in Oberlands Road, La Corbinerie, was formerly the German Fortress Commander's Bunker.

Below right: The control room in the Guernsey bunker.

Torteval

As well as the post on Alderney, there are a further three monitoring posts on Guernsey itself, similar in function to the underground monitoring posts found on the mainland until 1991, that report to the Guernsey Civil Protection headquarters. The posts are located at St Martin, Vale and Torteval, seen above.

These, and the Jersey monitoring posts at Gourey, Egypte, and St Ouen's Church, are normally unmanned and are provided with automatic radiation sensors which send data continuously to their respective control centres. The primary hazard anticipated on the islands is not nuclear war, but an accident at the French nuclear waste reprocessing plant near Cherbourg.

Above: The Torteval monitoring post, housed in a heavily-protected single-storey German telephone network junction bunker dating from the Second World War.

Left: An interior view of the Torteval bunker. The structure is very little changed from its wartime appearance and many German notices are still in evidence. It is the policy of the Civil Protection organisation to preserve these features as part of the island's wartime heritage.

Jersey

Above: The Jersey Civil Protection control is housed in a former German telephone repeater bunker on Trinity Road in St Helier. The two extensions visible on the roof contain air-conditioning plant and a standby generator.

Above right: At the bunker's entrance the original German gas-tight door visible in the foreground was supplemented in the 1980s by the massive blast-door seen behind.

Below: The BBC broadcasting studio in the Jersey bunker.

Below and opposite: Two interior views of the Jersey Civil Protection control room, still fully operational.

Chapter 10

TELECOMMUNICATIONS BUNKERS

If Britain was to survive the immediate aftermath of a nuclear war, the existence of a robust and resilient communications system would be essential to ensure the continuity of government. In the 1950s and 1960s the only system offering such resilience was the network of long-distance trunk cables that formed the core of the GPO telephone system. This system was essential, also, for the transmission of data from the RAF radar stations and for the dissemination of vital information by the United Kingdom Warning and Monitoring Organisation.

Whilst the buried GPO cables were relatively immune from disruption on their cross-country routes, they were dangerously exposed where they emerged at their nodal and terminal points. These were almost invariably trunk exchanges or repeater stations in or near the centres of cities that would be primary targets in the events of war.

To counter this threat, deep-level underground emergency telephone exchanges were built beneath London, Birmingham and Manchester, the three cities considered to be at the greatest risk. On the outskirts of Manchester and Birmingham, heavily protected semi-underground trunk repeater stations were built to provide alternative communication routes around the cities. Two each were provided at Manchester and Birmingham, along with four other hardened repeater stations at key points on the network.

Kingsway

As stated above, new tunnels were bored beneath Manchester and Birmingham but, in London, the Kingsway exchange was constructed in an existing tunnel system beneath Chancery Lane tube station. This was to have formed part of an abortive underground high-speed rail link.

The Chancery Lane tunnels were acquired by the Post Office under the Emergency Powers Act in 1949 and, in 1951, work began on construction of the Kingsway trunk exchange. During the construction stage, four additional tunnels were bored, running south from the existing pair of shelter tunnels, with interconnecting cross-passages and subsidiary service tunnels. Access to the underground complex was via passenger lifts in High Holborn and Took's Court, with a goods lift in Furnival Street. The exchange had emergency dormitory accommodation for its 150 operators and other staff and had its own artesian well to supply water.

By the 1980s the role of the Kingsway exchange had diminished significantly. For a short while, an area already declared redundant by British Telecom figured briefly in the Home Office emergency government scheme, but this came to an end prior to 1996. The whole site was redundant by 2008.

Above: The discreet entrance to the Kingsway exchange in the original, long-disused entrance to Chancery Lane tube station at 31-33 High Holborn.

Above: In an emergency situation the full 1.5 Megawatt load of the Kingsway exchange could be met by its own underground power station which contained three 500 KVA Ruston Hornsby alternator sets.

Left: Low-tension switchgear in the exchange sub-station. From here, current from the station's transformers is distributed to the various plant and service installations. The circuit-breaker labelled 'L.F.B. Airplant Shut Down Switch' is provided in order that, in the event of a fire underground, the London Fire Brigade can immediately shut down the exchange's ventilation fans.

Below left: High-voltage transformers in the sub-station's transformer hall.

Below right: Part of the Kingsway Exchange air-conditioning and ventilation system.

Opposite: A view of the Main Distribution Frame at Kingsway.

Left: The staff recreation room at Kingsway. The garish 1970s' décor has survived until the present day.

Below left: The junction of 'Main Alley' and the centre of 'South Street' in the underground exchange at Kingsway.

Below right: Blast-doors at the base of the High Holborn lift shaft.

PR1 & PR2 REPEATER STATIONS

The PR1 and PR2 protected repeater stations are similar structures, differing only in that the PR1 equipment rooms are some twenty feet shorter. They are double-level bunkers with the lower floor underground and with walls, roofs and floor slabs of eighteen-inch-thick reinforced concrete. A single-storey annexe provides office accommodation and is not blast-proofed.

At one end of the building a large concrete ventilation shaft descends through the upper floor into a sealed, ventilation plant-room on the lower floor. From this chamber outside air is drawn through banks of filters into an air-conditioning plant in the bunker's adjacent main plant-room. Also contained in the lower-floor plant-room are two standby generators, one to provide power for the telecommunications equipment and one for general station services. Two equipment rooms, one on the upper and one on the lower floor, contain the telecommunications equipment racks.

Stockport
Above: The Stockport PR1 repeater stands in Hempshaw Lane, Stockport.

Lyndon Green
Above: The Lyndon Green PR1 is located in Sheldon near Birmingham.

Portsmouth
Above: The PR1 bunker on Portsdown Hill, overlooking Portsmouth harbour.

Queslett (Birmingham)
Above: The Queslett PR1 bunker now houses the Beacon Telephone Exchange.

Warmley
Above: The PR2 bunker at Warmley, near Bristol, was demolished in 2001.

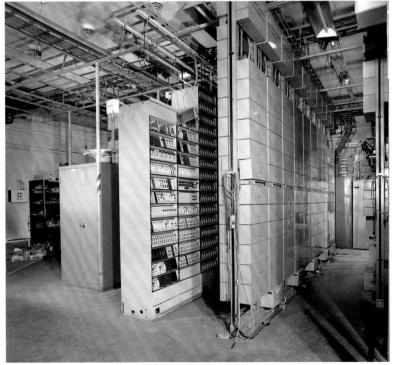

Rothwell Haigh

Above: The PR2 telephone repeater station at Rothwell Haigh, southeast of Leeds in Yorkshire. A smaller bunker nearby provided accommodation for the Central Electricity Generating Board's North East Region Emergency Grid Control Centre. A building control application to demolish the bunker was made to Leeds City Council in 2006.

Lyndon Green

Left: Apparatus racks in the lower-floor equipment room. The grey-cased equipment in the foreground dates from the 1950s or 60s; the cream-coloured repeaters in the background were probably installed in the 1980s.

Stockport

Opposite: A corner of the lower-floor equipment room at the Stockport PR2 repeater. The cylindrical objects on the foreground rack are tone generators. The dials on the rack in the background measure the pressure in the underground distribution cables. The cables are pressurised to keep out moisture, so a drop in pressure would indicate damage to the cable.

Stockport

Above: A pair of motor-generators in the upper-floor telecommunications plant-room at Stockport. Driven by mains AC motors, the generators provided low-voltage DC current to charge the station's batteries and to drive other communications equipment.

Warmley

Above: Generators in the lower-floor plant-room in the Warmley PR2 station. These were standby sets for use in case of a mains failure supply. One unit provided power to the station's telecommunications equipment via motor-generator sets like those shown opposite, while the other provided a 415 volt three-phase AC supply for general station services. The AC alternator would ensure the continuous operation of the station's air-conditioning plant.

Chapter 11

PUBLIC UTILITY BUNKERS

Although the GPO telecommunication system received the highest priority in the planning for the continuity of government in the event of a nuclear war, the other public utilities – all nationalised industries in the 1950s – also developed contingency plans at various times during the Cold War. The Central Electricity Generating Board, for example, was provided with national and regional emergency control centres from an early stage. In the early 1950s work began on the first of a proposed thirty emergency railway control centres, although only four of these had been built when the scheme was abandoned in 1956.

During the final phase of the Cold War, in the late 1980s, Home Office funding was given to the various soon-to-be-privatised water boards, and to the existing water companies, for the construction of emergency water control centres from which, it was hoped, the provision of adequate supplies of drinking water for the civil population could be overseen.

Brede Waterworks
Below: The Southern Water emergency control bunker at Brede waterworks in East Sussex is built into a hillside and looks very much like a typical, small reservoir, the only clue to its true function being the prominent ventilation shafts rising from its roof.

Above left and right: The air-filtration plant and standby generator in the Southern Water emergency bunker at Brede.

Burntisland

Below: The railway control bunker at Burntisland in Fife, one of the four bunkers built before the scheme was abandoned in 1956. The other three bunkers were at Bricket Wood, Knebworth and Huyton Junction.

Chatham Waterworks

Above: Southern Water's Chatham emergency control centre is actually located at Farthing Corner near Gillingham. Built within a disused covered reservoir, the bunker was completed but never fitted-out for use.

Below left: The Faraday Cage in the bunker's control room. It was intended that this should contain telephone switching equipment but this was never installed.

Below: The bunker's toilet facility, with distinctly daunting plumbing.

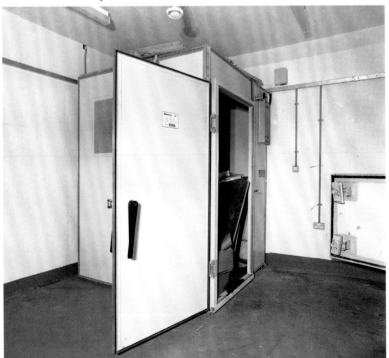

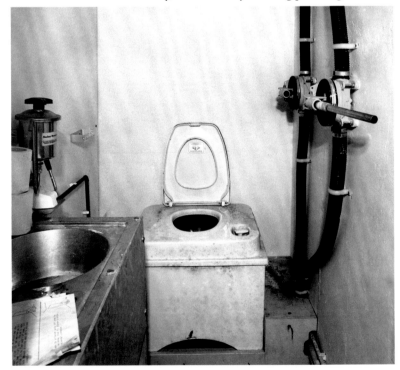

Nettlebridge Waterworks

Above: The Bristol Water Company's emergency control bunker was built within the shell of a disused Victorian reservoir in the Nettlebridge Valley near Radstock in Somerset. Construction started as late as 1989 but was abandoned before completion at the end of the Cold War.
Below: Air filtration plant in the Nettlebridge bunker.

Seven Trent Water HQ, Staverton near Gloucester

Above: Severn Trent Water's main emergency control centre is in the basement of their headquarters in Staverton. The windowless, plain brick wall to the left of the entrance conceals a concrete ventilation shaft rising from the basement to roof height.
Below: Massive concrete and steel blast-doors at the entrance to the bunker.

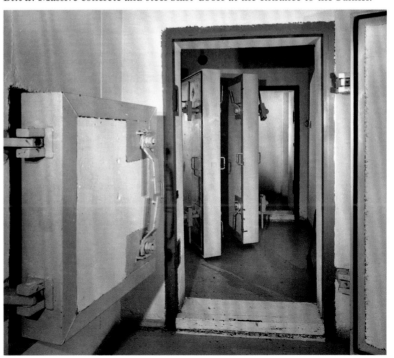

Totnes Waterworks

Above: The semi-underground South West Water emergency bunker at Little Hempston near Totnes in Devon. South West Water built two other emergency bunkers, one at Coswarth near Newquay and the other, built into the wall of a dam, at the Drift Reservoir near Penzance.

Below left: Air filtration equipment in the Totnes bunker. Note the hand-crank for use in the event of a power failure.

Below right: The Totnes control room, now disused except for rough storage. All the South West Water bunkers fell out of use at the end of the Cold War, although the one at the Drift Reservoir was later adapted as a pumping station.

Chapter 12

MILITARY CONTROL BUNKERS

Bentley Priory

The mansion at Bentley Priory, near Stanmore in Middlesex, was acquired by the Air Ministry in 1926 and in 1936 became the headquarters of the newly formed RAF Fighter Command. At the start of the Second World War a huge, two-level underground control centre was built some forty feet below the lawn of the house. This became operational in March 1940. From 1953 Bentley Priory also acted as an Air Defence Operations Centre (ADOC) for both Fighter and Bomber Commands. Following the formation of Strike Command in 1968, its operations centre moved to High Wycombe, leaving just the ADOC at Bentley Priory where it remained until its closure in 1971.

In 1979 plans were prepared for a new UKAIR Permanent Static War Headquarters at High Wycombe. After fifteen years under care and maintenance the bunker at Bentley Priory was refurbished and extended to provide a reserve, alternative site to High Wycombe. This task was completed in 1990. RAF Bentley Priory closed on 31 May 2008 and in September 2010 planning permission to redevelop the site was obtained which will include demolition of the bunker.

Below: The massive, blast-proof entrance to the Bentley Priory bunker.

During the reconstruction of the underground control centre at Bentley Priory, a completely new underground bunker was constructed nearby to house the necessary power, ventilation and air-conditioning plant rooms.

Above left: The entrance to the new plant-room bunker.

Above right: The new standby generator installed at Bentley Priory during the 1986-1990 refurbishment.

Left: A bank of air filters in the ventilation plant-room.

Opposite: Part of the very extensive air-conditioning plant installed at Bentley Priory.

Above: The secondary standby generator associated with the air-conditioning plant at Bentley Priory.

Left: Switchgear and control equipment in the plant-room.

Opposite: This console controlled access through the air-lock and decontamination suite at the entrance to the Bentley Priory bunker.

HMS *Wildfire*

In 1937, plans were made for protected Area Command Headquarters (ACHQ<u>s</u>) at the four Naval ports of Plymouth, Portsmouth, Chatham and Rosyth. The Chatham headquarters would accommodate the Commander in Chief, Nore Command, RN; the Air Officer Commanding, No.16 Group RAF Coastal Command, and a small Army contingent. Work began in May 1939 on the excavation of a series of tunnels to house the ACHQ beneath the chalk hills to the west of Admiralty House at Chatham. The task was completed in December 1939. Most of the tunnels were made to the size of standard mining hoops, the exception being the area in which the forty-foot-wide Central Plotting Room was constructed. Here, steel segments similar to those used in the London Underground were employed.

Nore Command was abolished in 1961 and the ACHQ closed the following year. Less than three years later, however, in 1964, the tunnels were refurbished and reopened as the Local Command Headquarters (LCHQ) for the Flag Officer, Medway. The headquarters became redundant in 1983 following the closure of the Chatham naval base. In recent years the site has suffered fire-damage and general vandalism. The bunker has now been permanently sealed as part of the redevelopment of the site.

Above left: The teleprinter room at HMS *Wildfire*.
Below left: Air filters, probably dating from the Second World War, in the ventilation plant.
Opposite: The Central Plotting Room.
Below right: A view from the balcony down on to the plotting table.

Daws Hill

The 23,000 square-foot underground bunker at RAF Daws Hill lies behind High Wycombe Abbey School. The base, which dates from the Second World War, was occupied by the United States Air Force which, after a brief post-war absence, returned to Daws Hill in 1953. Until 1963 it was an important command and communications centre for USAF nuclear bombers stationed in the United Kingdom. The bunker was refurbished in 1986 to function as the USAF Headquarters in Europe. Plans prepared for a cruise missile programming and data centre at Daws Hill were later abandoned. In recent years the site functioned primarily as a US storage facility until its closure in 2007.

Left: The discreet entrance to the Daws Hill bunker.

Below left: Blast-doors and air-lock inside the bunker's entrance building.

Below right: Exceptionally large air filters in the ventilation plant at Daws Hill.

Greenham Common

The first of the ninety-six cruise missiles based at RAF Greenham Common arrived in 1983. The missiles, and their associated mobile control centres, were stored on launcher vehicles in a group of six massively-hardened silos known as the Ground-Launched Cruise Missile Alert and Maintenance Area (GAMA).

Above: The lower, left-hand end of the administration building at Greenham Common contains the Missile Command Centre bunker. Its function was to relay final launch codes to the missile trailers which, in the event of a nuclear war, would have already relocated to their remote launch positions.

Left: Air filtration and ventilation equipment in the Command Centre plant-room.

Above: A view of the control room within the Command Centre. The sliding blackboards above the dais displayed status information about each of Greenham Common's missiles.

Mount Wise

In 1939 work began on the construction of a two-storey bomb-proof bunker in a ditch near Hamoaze House at Plymouth. The bunker, which was completed in 1941, functioned as the Headquarters of the Commander in Chief, Plymouth. It was greatly extended during the lead-up to D-Day by excavating a series of tunnels, known as The Plymouth Underground Extension, beneath the lawn of nearby Admiralty House. These tunnels provided space for a tactical communications facility.

In the post-war years, the bunker, now known as the Plymouth Maritime Headquarters, was considerably upgraded, but by the 1980s was approaching obsolescence.

In 1991 a major reconstruction was completed which included the building of a new, third-floor plant-room extension. By 2004, however, the whole site was redundant and being prepared for disposal.

Left: The main entrance to the Plymouth Maritime Headquarters.

Below left and right: Two views of the British Telecom frame room in the bunker's communications area.

Above: A view along the roofline of the Mount Wise bunker. The concrete extensions, with grilled openings, are air inlets for the new ventilation plant-room constructed between 1990 and 1991.

Below: By 2004 most of the movable fixtures and equipment had been removed from the bunker prior to its planned disposal. These large wall-maps, however, remained.

Above: Compressors and condensers in the new plant-room extension at the Plymouth Maritime Headquarters.

Below: Part of the bunker's ventilation equipment.

Above: External cooling units for the high-voltage transformers in the Mount Wise bunker.

Below: One of three emergency exit tunnels that emerge onto the foreshore from the Plymouth Underground Extension.

Strike Command Defence Headquarters, High Wycombe

Right: During the late 1970s a tunnel built during the Second World War, joining two buildings at Bomber Command Headquarters at High Wycombe, was adapted as a Defence Headquarters for RAF Strike Command, the current incumbent. Its principal role was to co-ordinate the local defence of Strike Command Headquarters in the event of an emergency.

Henley-on-Thames

During the Second World War, two disused underground chalk quarries near Henley-on-Thames, each extending to about 30,000 square feet, were converted into underground aircraft-component factories. Subsequently one of these, at Warren Row, became an RSG, famously exposed by *Spies for Peace* in 1963. The other, near Park Place School, became the Armed Forces Headquarters for No.6 Region in 1985. Previously, since 1974, the AFHQ had been located in the former RSG at Warren Row.

Below left: The main access tunnel to the Park Place bunker at Henley-on-Thames, looking little changed from its wartime appearance.

Below right: Abandoned manual switchboards in the communications centre of the Armed Forces Headquarters.

Wilton Park

In 1954 work began on the construction of an extensive new bunker at Wilton Park near Beaconsfield in Buckinghamshire. The bunker was to jointly accommodate Eastern Command Army Headquarters, the London District Army War Headquarters and an Army communications centre. A few years later the Regional Army Commands were relocated to the Regional Seats of Government and the role of the Wilton bunker consequently diminished. The end of the RSG organisation in 1967, however, saw the return of the Armed Forces Headquarters to Wilton Park.

A planned upgrade in the 1980s does not appear to have been completed. At that time the bunker also housed the Thames Valley Flood Co-ordination Headquarters, which remained there until it was made redundant by the Thames Barrier in 1984.

Above: The grey bulk of the Wilton Park bunker, prominent amongst the other buildings on the site in this oblique aerial view.

Left and overleaf: Following its closure in the 1980s, the plant-room, which is on a slightly lower level than the main part of the bunker, has been subject to serious flooding.

Chapter 13

CENTRAL GOVERNMENT WAR HEADQUARTERS

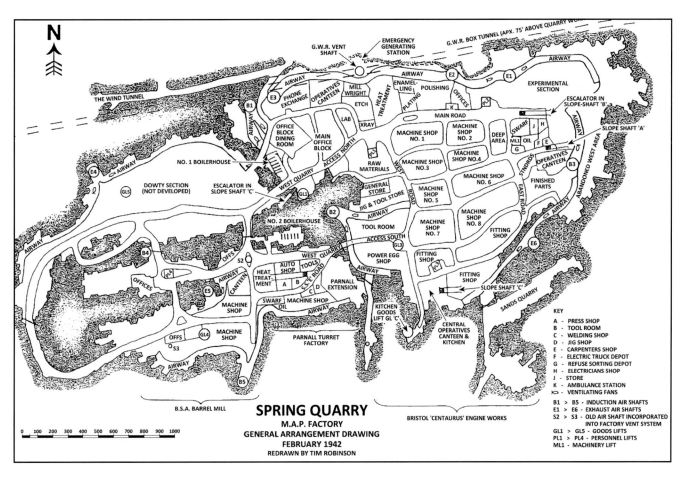

SPRING QUARRY
M.A.P. FACTORY
GENERAL ARRANGEMENT DRAWING
FEBRUARY 1942
REDRAWN BY TIM ROBINSON

Throughout the Second World War the British Government exhibited a dogged determination to remain in London whatever the risks such a course of action might present. The same determination appears to have prevailed during the early post-war years, when tension between the Western Powers and the Soviet Union threatened a new conflict in Europe. Even the prospect of a city laid waste by atomic bombs could not convince the Cabinet that a safe, alternative refuge, far from London, would be desirable. Plans were, therefore, prepared in the early 1950s for a proliferation of new bunkers and tunnels, deep below the streets and basements of Westminster, to protect the nucleus of government in the event of war.

There were, however, cautious voices within the Civil Service suggesting that other proposals should be considered for an alternative seat of government,

in an area remote from the Capital. There is evidence that a prospective site at Corsham, in north Wiltshire, had been earmarked for such a purpose from as early as 1946. In September of that year Mr A K Davis, a civil servant at the Ministry of Supply tasked with the disposal of a number of wartime factories and warehouses, when asked to review files relating to the former Bristol Aeroplane Company's underground factory at Spring Quarry in Corsham, commented: 'I can find no aspect of factory disposal in them, in fact I gather that the policy is to hold on firmly to our best refuge from the atom bomb.'

Construction of the seventy-six-acre underground factory at Spring Quarry had begun in November, 1940, and was still unfinished when the war ended. The factory, which was intended to offer alternative, bomb-proof accommodation for the Bristol Aeroplane Company's aircraft-engine production facility (then

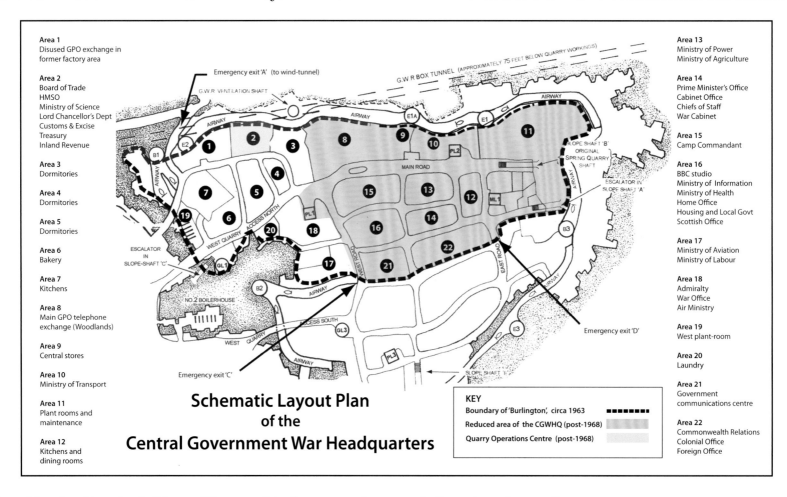

Area 1
Disused GPO exchange in
former factory area

Area 2
Board of Trade
HMSO
Ministry of Science
Lord Chancellor's Dept
Customs & Excise
Treasury
Inland Revenue

Area 3
Dormitories

Area 4
Dormitories

Area 5
Dormitories

Area 6
Bakery

Area 7
Kitchens

Area 8
Main GPO telephone
exchange (Woodlands)

Area 9
Central stores

Area 10
Ministry of Transport

Area 11
Plant rooms and
maintenance

Area 12
Kitchens and
dining rooms

Area 13
Ministry of Power
Ministry of Agriculture

Area 14
Prime Minister's Office
Cabinet Office
Chiefs of Staff
War Cabinet

Area 15
Camp Commandant

Area 16
BBC studio
Ministry of Information
Ministry of Health
Home Office
Housing and Local Govt
Scottish Office

Area 17
Ministry of Aviation
Ministry of Labour

Area 18
Admiralty
War Office
Air Ministry

Area 19
West plant-room

Area 20
Laundry

Area 21
Government
communications centre

Area 22
Commonwealth Relations
Colonial Office
Foreign Office

**Schematic Layout Plan
of the
Central Government War Headquarters**

KEY
Boundary of 'Burlington', circa 1963 ▪▪▪▪▪▪▪▪
Reduced area of the CGWHQ (post-1968)
Quarry Operations Centre (post-1968)

located in vulnerable surface buildings at Filton, near Bristol) was expected to be completed within six months, at an estimated cost of £100,000. The project was, however, far too ambitious and, due principally to the 'costs-plus-profit' contracts under which it was financed, open to charges of corruption. The final cost of construction was in excess of £13,000,000, yet only a handful of engines were ever produced there.

Although the factory was hopelessly inefficient and widely regarded as a white-elephant, its infrastructure was prodigious. Built almost 100 feet below ground in a disused stone quarry, the factory was accessed by four high-speed passenger lifts, five goods lifts, two twenty-ton machinery lifts and two Otis escalators that had been requisitioned in 1941 from the London Transport tube stations at St. Paul's and Holborn. There was also a smaller lift used solely to replenish the underground canteens, and a number of inclined shafts for use as pedestrian emergency exits. Ventilation was by means of fourteen air-shafts and at least a dozen high-capacity circulating fans. Two underground boilerhouses, each with six Lancashire boilers, provided process and heating steam for the factory. Given the level of protection it offered, the fact that it was well-provided with sewerage, water and gas services, had its own dedicated GPO telephone exchange underground and boasted a robust electricity distribution system, there can be little wonder that it attracted the attention of those seeking

a site for an alternative seat of government.

In July 1951, the Committee on Distribution of Government Staffs in War discussed the possibility of an alternative seat of government should London become untenable, and was told of the potential suitability of the Corsham complex. Plans for the quarry, (by now codenamed SUBTERFUGE), were considered throughout 1952 and 1953 but the consensus remained that any remote, alternative headquarters should be secondary to London and that the proposed Whitehall tunnel scheme should continue. Even as late as October 1953, the influential Working Party on the Machinery of Government in War, under the chairmanship of Sir Thomas Padmore, was of the opinion that the nucleus of government should remain in London and that SUBTERFUGE should be a subordinate body reporting to it. By the end of the following year, however, Padmore's group had reassessed its conclusions in the light of scientific evidence concerning the effects of radioactive fallout. It now concluded that the government nucleus should evacuate to SUBTERFUGE in the first instance, and that the majority of Whitehall's civil servants should disperse at a later date as circumstances dictated. In January 1955, the Cabinet agreed in general with Padmore's scheme, although the Home Defence Committee muddied the waters by suggesting that the disused underground factory at Drakelow near Kidderminster should be the location of the alternative seat of government, rather than Spring Quarry at Corsham. Arguments concerning the use of Drakelow as an alternative to, or in conjunction with, the Spring Quarry site were to re-emerge regularly, in various forms, for many years.

Eventually, in September 1955, the SUBTERFUGE scheme was formally approved by Prime Minister Anthony Eden, and the Ministry of Works was instructed to prepare the necessary construction contracts. The main infrastructure cost, excluding communications equipment or any fixtures and fittings, was estimated at £1,200,000, and construction was expected to take three years to complete. Initial plans were based upon the assumption that the headquarters would house a complement of 4,000 civil servants including key decision-makers and their support staff. Of these, more than 1,000 would be directly involved with communications. Stringent efforts were later made to reduce the total staffing level to below 4,000.

Building work began in July 1956 and by the summer of 1959 was two-thirds complete. None of the communications equipment had yet been installed but it was thought that, in an emergency, the bunker could operate in a limited role. Due principally to funding constraints, construction, and the installation by the GPO of the headquarters' enormously complex telephone and teleprinter systems, proceeded only slowly and was not completed until August 1962.

The bunker, known officially as the Central Government War Headquarters (CGWHQ), occupies a nineteen-acre section of the former factory situated in the northeast sector of the quarry adjacent to Box railway tunnel. This area was segregated from the rest of the quarry by four-feet-thick concrete walls. The existing layout of factory roadways was maintained largely in its original form. Similarly, the existing layout of workshops and storage areas was retained, although adapted and subdivided to provide the necessary offices for the various government departments and ancillary facilities. Much of the original factory ventilation plant was retained although its mode of operation underwent a radical alteration. The existing boilerhouse and steam-heating system, which was anyway obsolete, was taken out of use, the temperature in the headquarters being maintained instead by the recovery of waste heat from a pair of newly installed Sultzer dehumidifiers. Near the ventilation shafts, electrostatic precipitation filters were installed to cleanse the incoming air.

The CGWHQ had existed for little more than two years before questions were asked concerning its fitness for purpose. By 1964, proposals were being developed that envisioned a dispersed, rather than centralised, form of emergency government, with the existing Corsham headquarters utilised as a post-attack accretion centre. Under these plans, the staffing level at the bunker, known by 1968 as TURNSTILE, was reduced to no more than 1,000. This reduction in numbers facilitated a reduction in the physical size of the bunker, allowing nine discreet 'Areas' at the western end of the quarry to be abandoned, along with most of the catering and other plant installed there.

Virtually disused by 1991, the CGWHQ's functional utility came to an official end in 1999. Five years later, in December 2004, an MoD press release announced that: 'A formerly secret government underground site near Corsham in Wiltshire, which was a potential relocation site for the Government in the event of a nuclear war, was declassified at the end of 2004'.

Above: The earth-mounded, blast-protected shaft-top building for passenger lift PL1, beside Westwells Road in Corsham.

Above: The interior of the entrance air-lock in the PL1 shaft-top building.

Above: The lower lift landing of PL1, with the doors of the left-hand car open. This equipment has remained unchanged since it was installed in 1941.

Above: This broad underground roadway, known as 'Main Road', runs from west to east; it joins passenger lift PL1 and escalator 'C' at the west end of the site with PL2 and the service area, at the east end. This view is looking east at the approach to Area 9.

Left: The lower landing of passenger lift PL2. Note the original panelling in the lift-car, and the brass rotary controllers which date from the time when the lifts were installed by the Ministry of Aircraft Production in 1941.

Opposite: The top flight of a pair of escalators in slope-shaft 'C', at the west end of the quarry. The lower escalator was installed in 1942 as part of the Spring Quarry factory project. The upper extension was installed in the early 1960s to supplement an existing stairway. The escalators have been disused for many years.

Above: The former London Transport escalator in slope shaft 'A', at the east end of the quarry. Although no longer used as an escalator, it has been locked in position as a fixed stairway and functions as an emergency exit route.

Above: The map room in Area 14. A range of large windows at the end of this
room, behind the camera, overlooks the Cabinet Office conference room.

Area 8 houses the headquarters' main telephone exchange, together with a GPO repeater station and a teleprinter exchange.

Left: Two magnificent manual switchboards were installed in the GPO telephone exchange. The fourteen-position unit shown here was dedicated primarily to international communications.

Left: The exchange supervisor's and directory enquiry desks, adjacent to the main switchboard. The telephone directories date from 1988.

Opposite: The forty-position main GPO switchboard.

Above: Part of the Main Distribution Frame in the GPO exchange.
Below: Public address amplifiers in Area 15. This equipment, probably dating from the factory era, was used for internal communication.

Above: Telegraph switching equipment in the exchange frame-room.

Below: The BBC studio in Area 16.

Above: Teleprinters and other telegraph instruments in Area 16.

Above: The twenty-four station Lamson tube exchange, located in Area 15.

Above: The Mason automatic bread-machine which was installed in the bakery in Area 6 in the early 1960s. Areas 6 and 7, and most of the industrial catering equipment contained within them, were abandoned in 1968 when the scope and role of the Corsham headquarters was drastically reduced.

Although, under the original Corsham scheme, there were extensive kitchens and bakeries established in Areas 7 and 8, at the west end of the quarry, by 1968 all the catering facilities were concentrated at the east end, in Area 12.

Left: The double-fronted tea bar in Area 12, showing two Stott coffee machines mounted on the counters and, in the background, an electric tea urn.

Left: A wider view of the tea bar showing the seating arrangements.

Opposite: The servery for the central canteen in Area 12.

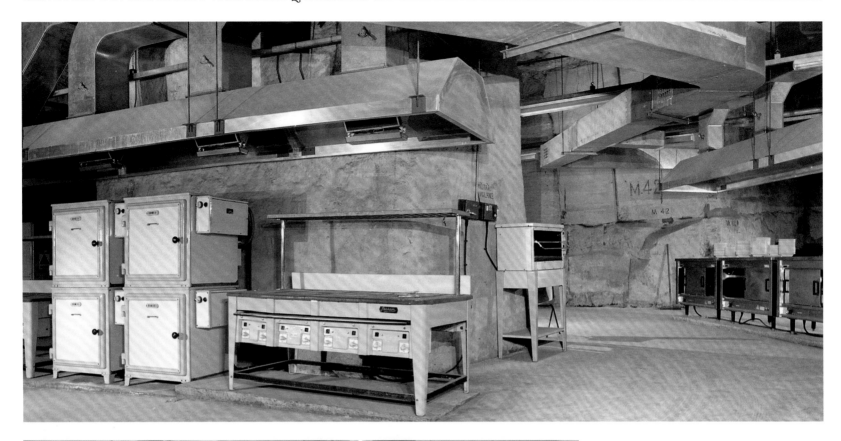

Above and left: Industrial catering equipment, most of which dates from the 1960s, in the Area 12 kitchens.

Opposite: The Sulzer air-conditioning plant, located at the east end of the quarry in Area 11. This equipment, which operated in a similar way to a domestic refrigerator, produced chilled water for the quarry's dehumidification and air-washing plant. Waste heat from the Sulzer unit was recirculated to heat the entire headquarters.

A similar plant was installed in Area 19 at the west end of the quarry, but was abandoned in 1968.

Above: Two of the four Mirrlees JVSS12 diesel generator sets installed in the headquarters' underground power station. The power station occupies the site of the former factory's No.1 boiler house, which originally contained six Lancashire boilers in three groups of two. Four boilers were removed to make way for the generator sets; the other two survive, but devoid of all their gauges, cocks, and other fittings.

Above: The Quarry Operations Centre (QOC) in Area 2. Established in an area previously occupied by the Board of Trade and other government finance departments, the QOC offered protected accommodation for RAF personnel on the Corsham site. Provided with its own armoury, it also served as a co-ordination centre for local ground defence.

Chapter 14

LOCAL AUTHORITY BUNKERS

The reconstitution of the Civil Defence Corps in 1948, just three years after its abolition at the end of the Second World War, saw Britain's local authorities once again charged with responsibility for co-ordinating local resources and overseeing rescue and recovery operations in the event of war. Throughout the Cold War, and particularly after the final winding-down of the Civil Defence Corps in 1968, the local authorities found themselves burdened with ever-increasing responsibilities as the Central and Regional Governments delegated power down to County and District levels. Following the revival of Emergency Planning in the early 1980s (after a lull during the previous decade) some councils embraced the process wholeheartedly, building lavish new emergency centres below their County Halls and Civic Centres, while others paid little more than lip-service.

In the post-Cold-War world, many of these bunkers have taken on a more general civil emergencies role; others have simply been abandoned.

Bedminster

Opposite: Constructed in 1938, during the pre-war build-up of Civil Defence, the bunker in Banwell Close, Bedminster, was one of four Bristol Civil Defence Sub-Controls. After a short post-war period under various tenants, it was reopened as a Civil Defence control from the mid-1950s until 1968.

Above: The control room of the Bedminster bunker, with the resource board and other artefacts still in place. After the abolition of the Civil Defence Corps in 1968, the building was locked-up and forgotten about for over thirty years. Many of its fixtures and fittings, including the standby generator and ventilation system, survived until the bunker was demolished in 2005.

Left: Some years after its closure, the plot of land upon which the Bitterne bunker was built was incorporated into the garden of a nearby private house. The building was maintained in good order, serving as a garden shed and general storeroom. Although the house still stands, the plot of land at the end of the garden was sold for redevelopment in the late 2000s and the bunker has been demolished.

Bitterne

Southampton's eastern Civil Defence Sub-Control, near the junction of Somerset Avenue and Bitterne Road, was opened in September 1955. Its working life ended in 1968 following the winding-up of the Civil Defence organisation.

Right: The control room of the Bitterne bunker. Although stripped of most of its original contents, the resource board has survived. Note the emergency exit in the rear wall.

Camden The Camden Borough Control is situated in a small park near the junction of Highgate Road and Gordon House Road. It opened in 1953, reporting to the Mill Hill War Room.

Above left and right: Sealed and forgotten since its closure in 1968, the Camden bunker has suffered considerable damage due to the effects of damp. Most of the timber partitions have collapsed.

Cornwall

Left: The Cornwall County Emergency Centre was constructed in the basement of County Hall in Truro in 1982. It was built with little or no blast-protection. The facilities it would require in order to make it suitable for operation under closed-down conditions for a prolonged period, including its kitchen, dormitory and ventilation plant, were removed several years ago.

The centre consists of one large room, subdivided to form an operations room and a smaller communications room. The latter includes a small BBC studio, although this is not sound-proofed.

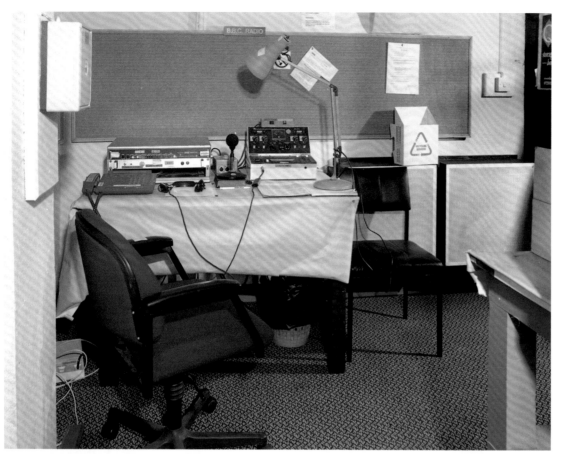

East Cambridge

The East Cambridge District Council Emergency Centre is situated in the basement of 'The Grange', a former maternity hospital in Nutholt Lane, Ely, that was converted into council offices in the early 1980s.

Left: The East Cambridge bunker, like the Cornwall County Emergency Centre, is one of just a few local authority bunkers provided with rudimentary BBC radio studios.

Edmonton

Below left: Access to the Edmonton Borough Control was via an anonymous door adjacent to the main entrance of the Plevna Road Clinic in Edmonton. The bunker was constructed in the basement of the clinic when it was built in 1958.

Below right: The communications room at Edmonton. Plans to refurbish the bunker in 1989 were abandoned when it was found impossible to control the ingress of water.

Edmonton

Above: Edmonton's standby generator, submerged in two feet of putrid seepage water. The Plevna Road Clinic, and the bunker beneath, were demolished in 2008 to make way for an Asda superstore.

Epping

Opposite: The Epping Forest District Council emergency centre was located in the Second World War RAF Sector Operations Centre at North Weald Airfield in Essex.

Right: The control room at Epping. The bunker was partially rebuilt internally in 1986 and continued in service until the mid-1990s. Connection to the Emergency Communication Network was maintained until at least 2000 and a RAYNET (Radio Amateurs' Emergency Network) group remained based at the bunker for some years. Once the RAYNET group departed, however, the site was broken into and vandalised. Demolition followed in 2007.

Fareham

Below: Now abandoned and disused, the Fareham Borough Emergency Centre was built in the early 1980s in three Victorian, vaulted ammunition magazines in the southwest caponier of Fort Fareham.

Finsbury

Below: The two-level Finsbury Borough Control, located beneath Garnault Place near Finsbury Town Hall, was flooded to the top of the stairs between the two floors. This is one of the rooms on the lower floor after the water was pumped out.

Hackney

Above right: The Hackney Borough Control started life in 1939 as the Borough's ARP Control Centre. Located beneath a car park at the rear of Hackney Town Hall, access to the bunker is via a small concrete blockhouse that protects a dog-leg stairway. The underground accommodation consists of four principal rooms connected by an open corridor, together with a group of toilet cubicles.

The ARP control was abandoned at the end of the war, but was reactivated in 1952 to serve as the Borough Civil Defence Control. Percolating damp was a continuous problem, and in 1964 it was decided to abandon the Hackney bunker and co-locate the Hackney Control with the Stoke Newington Borough Control at Stoke Newington Town Hall. The following year the two boroughs merged.

Below right: The control room at Hackney, showing the effects of the pervading damp. Note the emergency exit high in the right-hand wall, accessed by a short steel ladder. Although there are several inches of water on the floor in places, the bunker is still used by the local authority for rough storage.

Opposite: Sutcliffe Speakman activated-charcoal air filters in the ventilation plant at Hackney. The 'bicycle' units visible in this photograph would be used to drive the ventilation plant manually in the event of a power failure.

Halifax

The Halifax County Borough Sub-Control was located beneath the bus garage in Skircoats Road in Halifax. Built as a tramshed in 1902, the building is supported upon a basement consisting of a series of vaulted tunnels. During the Second World War these tunnels were adapted to serve as a Civil Defence Centre, probably under the aegis of the bus operators, Halifax Corporation, as part of the Industrial Civil Defence scheme. Following years of disuse, the bunker was reactivated as the Halifax County Borough Sub-Control from 1964 until 1968.

Above left: The external entrance to the Halifax bunker, with the rebuilt bus garage visible in the background. Four emergency exits, all now blocked, emerged inside the garage at the bottom of vehicle inspection pits.

Above right: The 'Civil Defence Ambulance Service' sign on the wall dates from the Second World War.

Below right: Although partially refitted in 1978, the bunker was never used on account of its propensity to flooding. The effects of damp are clearly visible in this photograph of the tunnels, taken in 2001.

Kings Lynn

Above left: The dual-use Norfolk County Standby Control and West Norfolk District Control was built below the grounds of the Woodlands Nursing Home in South Wootton in 1966. Access was by means of a discreet wooden door in a lean-to extension attached to the front of the nursing home.

Above right: The bunker fell out of use in 1968 but was recommissioned and refitted in 1986, when the new air filters, seen here, were installed.

Right: Since the end of the Cold War the bunker has been abandoned and largely stripped of its moveable artefacts. The sign, seen here, on the wall of the unisex shower and toilet, is, however, a poignant survivor.

USE OF THESE TOILET, WATER SUPPLY & SINK FACILITIES, & DUMPING OF WASTE FLUIDS IN THE SUMP ARE STRICTLY FORBIDDEN AT ANY TIME PRECEDING A REAL NUCLEAR ATTACK WARNING.

MAINS FACILITIES ARE AVAILABLE ON THE GROUND FLOOR ABOVE.

Raigmore

The Highland Council Emergency Centre is located in the filter room of the Second World War RAF No.13 Group Sector Operations Centre at Raigmore, to the east of Inverness. The bunker was acquired by Highland Council in 1988 and refurbished (with the aid of a 90% Home Office grant) at a cost of £5,000,000.

Between 1958 and 1968 the bunker had been used by the Civil Defence Corps with little alteration from its wartime state. Thereafter, up until shortly before its purchase by the council, it had been occupied by the ROC as additional accommodation for its Group Control which was established in the nearby Second World War control bunker.

Above left: The control room at Raigmore, showing the high standard of finish achieved in the 1980s' refurbishment.

Left: The Raigmore communications centre.

Opposite: The new ventilation and air filtration plant installed at the Highland Council Emergency Centre in 1988. The racing bicycles, devoid of front wheels but otherwise complete with gears and rear brakes, are used to drive the ventilation fans in the event of a power failure.

Southwark

Above: The flooded communications room in the Southwark Borough Control. Located deep below a health centre, opposite Southwark Town Hall, the bunker was abandoned at the end of the Cold War and shortly afterwards the derelict health centre above was demolished. The bunker remains largely intact, although subject to the increasingly rapid ingress of seepage water.

Chapter 15

PRIVATE BUNKERS

Pluckley
Above: This surreal addition to the garden of Prebbles Hill Cottage in Pluckley, Kent, is all that is visible of a nuclear bunker buried beneath the lawn.

Above left: An interior view of the domestic shelter at Pluckley. Looking very much like a discarded decompression chamber, the bunker, which was put in place in 1962, is, in fact, a commercially manufactured, prefabricated concrete unit marketed by Fallout Shelters (Deal) Ltd. According to the manufacturers advertising material, 'this is essentially a fringe shelter by our standards, although it is heavier and able to withstand greater stresses than most frontline continental shelters. It is considered 95% safe against nuclear hazards at 6.5-7 miles from ground zero of a 10-15 megaton bomb.'

Brixham

Above right: A much more sophisticated bunker was incorporated into the structure of a newly-built house in Brixham in Devon. The two-storey house is built into a hillside with the bunker buried in the ground below. The basic structure consists of one-and-a-half steel containers welded together and encased in six feet of reinforced concrete. The main entrance, seen here, is accessed via a door in the back of a wardrobe in a lower-floor bedroom.

Below right: A gas-tight door in the main room of the bunker gives access to a vertical emergency exit shaft. This emerges through the floor of a utility room in the upper-floor of the house, and is secured at the top by a massive, hydraulically operated horizontal blast-door. A second escape shaft leads to another similar blast-door buried beneath a flower bed in the garden.

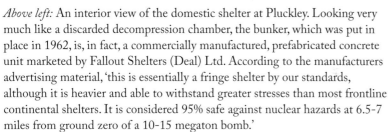

Balcombe

Above: The plant-room of a domestic nuclear shelter attached to a private house in Balcombe, near Haywards Heath in West Sussex. The bunker was constructed at a cost of £250,000 in 1982. It was built as a prototype for what the developer hoped would be a commercially saleable product but, in the end, only two examples of the design were ever sold.

BIBLIOGRAPHY

Beard, T and Emmerson A, 2007, *London's Secret Tubes*, Capital Transport Publishing, ISBN: 9781854143112

Campbell, D, 1982, *War Plan UK*, Burnett Books, ISBN: 9780091506711

Campbell, D, 1986, *The Unsinkable Aircraft Carrier*, Grafton Books, ISBN: 9780586086261

Clarke, R, 1986, *London Under Attack: The Report of the Greater London Area War Risk Study Commission*, Wiley-Blackwell, ISBN: 9780631150442

Cocroft, W D and Thomas, R J C, 2003, *Cold War: Building for Nuclear Confrontation 1946-89*, English Heritage, ISBN: 9781873592816

Dewar M, 1989, *Defence of the Nation*, Arms and Armour Press, ISBN: 9780853688365

Fox, S, *Control Chain*, Published privately

Fox, S, *Plan for Survival*, Published privately

Fox, S, 2010, 'Top Secret - Acid: The Story of the Central Government War Headquarters', *Subterranea*, Issue 22, 1 - 72, ISSN 1741-8917

Gough, J, 1992, *Watching the Skies*, HMSO, ISBN: 9780117727236

Home Office, *Emergency Planning Guidance to Local Authorities*

Home Office, 1980, *Protect and Survive*

Laurie, P, 1979, *Beneath the City Streets*, Panther, ISBN: 9780586050552

Martin, R H G, 2003, *A View of Air Defence Planning 1949-1964*, Richard H G Martin, ISBN: 9780954601706

McCamley, N, 2007, *Cold War Secret Nuclear Bunkers*, Pen & Sword Military, ISBN: 9781844155088

Spaven, M, 1983, *Fortress Scotland*, Pluto Press, ISBN: 9780861047352

Spies for Peace, 1963, *Danger! Official Secret RSG-6*

Stokes, P, 1996, *Drakelow Unearthed*, BCS/Paul Stokes, ISBN: 9780904015409

Wood, D, 1992, *Attack Warning Red*, Carmichael & Sweet Ltd, ISBN: 9780951728314

ACKNOWLEDGEMENTS

I would like to offer my thanks to Martin Dixon and Bob Jenner who helped with the proof reading, to Steve Fox for the picture on page 17 *(top left)*, and to Keith Ward for the picture on page 17 *(top right)*. My thanks, also, to Tim Robinson for redrawing the 1942 plan of Spring Quarry reproduced on page 181.